PHOTOGRAPHS BY EDWARD ADDEO

THE KITCHEN SLEUTH

IRRESISTIBLE RECIPES &
HOW THEY WERE DISCOVERED

By Henry A. Lambert

with Douglas Parreira

TABLE OF CONTENTS

FOREWORD

WHEN HENRY LAMBERT opened his first Pasta & Cheese shop in New York City, arugula was an alien green; mesclun had not even been invented yet. Brie was considered the ultimate in cheese sophistication, and "Parmesan" came mostly in green canisters. Mueller's was actually a leading dried pasta brand, and anyone who wanted fresh fettucine or ravioli had to schlep to Little Italy, the one in Manhattan or the one on Arthur Avenue. Pesto was a decade away from becoming the sauce in every pot, and flourless chocolate cake would have been passed off as a failed brownie.

Henry was so far ahead of the curve that he produced the first refrigerated pastas and sauces in America and went on to sell his company to Nestle in 1985 (the products are now available in supermarkets as Buitoni). But he did not lose his obsession with new food and innovative cooking, or his curiosity about how the best dishes in the best restaurants come together.

Henry, who also ran the restaurants at Bergdorf Goodman for 27 years, and whose Gotham salad remains a bestseller there, continued studying, including with Giuliano Bugialli. He has cajoled recipes out of chefs and restaurateurs and generally taken kitchen epiphanies and made them his own.

He met his collaborator Douglas Parreira while buying smoked salmon at Eli's down the block and asking for a lesson in how to slice, and they wound up putting in several hundred sessions together cooking the recipes in this book. (It was, Henry says, like having a trainer, but in the kitchen.) And he did all this while working nonstop as a real estate developer, with projects from Panama to Provence giving him even more opportunities to expand his repertoire.

Always, Henry wanted not just to taste new dishes but to dissect them, for the purpose of sharing. This self-styled kitchen sleuth developed no end of techniques to learn. Fortunately, most chefs and restaurateurs were kind enough to unriddle the recipes.

The 109 recipes in this book are his time-honored, repeatedly tested favorites, for dishes he makes when he's cooking for himself or, more often, for company. Ingredients such as sriracha and piment d'Espelette and kimchi would have been unimaginable to a Pasta & Cheese customer in the Eighties. But the fact that they are as common as ketchup in American supermarkets can be traced at least partly to a detective's approach to food.

~Regina Schrambling

INTRODUCTION

THE ENTICEMENT of a good meal is understood by the suitor, the salesman, the parent looking for a reason to gather a family to share time together. In collecting these recipes, I understood that this has motivated many who cook. Having started a food company, Pasta & Cheese, and having developed and owned several restaurants, including the three at Bergdorf Goodman and the Marguery Grill in New York, I have had the opportunity to learn from many cooks and to acquire many exceptional recipes.

Originally I wanted to study with James Beard, years ago, but his classes were full, so I signed on with Maurice Moore Betty. He was a very good teacher (and I say that not least because he thought I was one of his better students because I went on to open the Pasta & Cheese chain of stores that was the first company to sell refrigerated pastas and sauces in America, which are now called Buitoni in supermarkets — I was a student who made something of my training). All the recipes in Maurice Moore Betty's book are very good, particularly his dill sauce for gravlax, which is included in this collection.

Studying Viennese baking with Lilly Joss Reich was also helpful in my development as a cook. However, I learned the most in developing recipes for Pasta & Cheese, which I started in the Eighties, before the whole cheese trend, and for the restaurants at Bergdorf Goodman, which I ran for 27 years. I also learned from owning the Marguery Grill on East 65th Street. It got two stars from The New York Times; however, we lost $300,000 that year. It was doing very well until Joan Rivers was quoted as saying the food was terrific but everyone looked moribund in the restaurant.

Even earlier, I was responsible for renovating the Grand-Hotel du Cap-Ferrat on the French Riviera when I was president of the

Continued on page 10

Continued from page 9

Reliance Development Group. They used to joke about the fact that the previous people who had shown up to review the hotel's performance would only want to look at the sales figures while I would say, "Let me see the recipes."

Many restaurants have been willing to share recipes, and friends, such as Giuliano Bugialli and Pierre Mondard, each in his own right a star chef, were invaluable in developing recipes. This book is a continuation of the recipes that I have collected and developed since the completion of the Pasta & Cheese cookbook. Many of the recipes come from others, however most were developed in cooking over several years with Douglas Parreira, who has great talent and is now working as a private chef. Cheryl Chrysler was invaluable in rewriting the recipes, and Regina Schrambling was the editor who made the project into a readable book. My assistant Terri Canderozzi also made so many contributions in every way. Steven Jenkins contributed olive oil advice, and James Coogan offered cheese tips. Edward Addeo took the photographs and Gina Provenzano styled the food on a tight deadline with great results; Albert Chiang as art director brought the project to visual fruition.

I look forward to sharing this set of recipes with others who I hope will enjoy them as much as I do.

~Henry A. Lambert

"IT'S THE LAST 30 SECONDS THAT MAKE THE BIGGEST DIFFERENCE"

WHEN I STARTED AND RAN Pasta & Cheese in the Eighties, our food science consultant, Dr. Guy Livingston, always insisted on using the organoleptic test in evaluating a dish, which is the combination of how food looked, smelled and tasted. In developing recipes I have always kept this in mind. It has also helped me in trying to learn to replicate the dishes I most enjoyed eating. The visual presentation of a dish should not be overlooked.

Take the simple act of forming a slice of smoked salmon into a rosette for an hors d'oeuvre. Guests immediately want to touch it to eat it. Adding a few chives to the salmon immediately makes it more enticing. Light decoration makes a tremendous difference. An attractive presentation is very important.

Creating an enjoyable meal starts with good recipes that take advantage of when ingredients are at their best.

Picking the right cuts of meat or the vegetable or fruit that is ripe and vibrant makes a world of different. Even at Fresh Direct, everyone can't get the first cut.

~H. L.

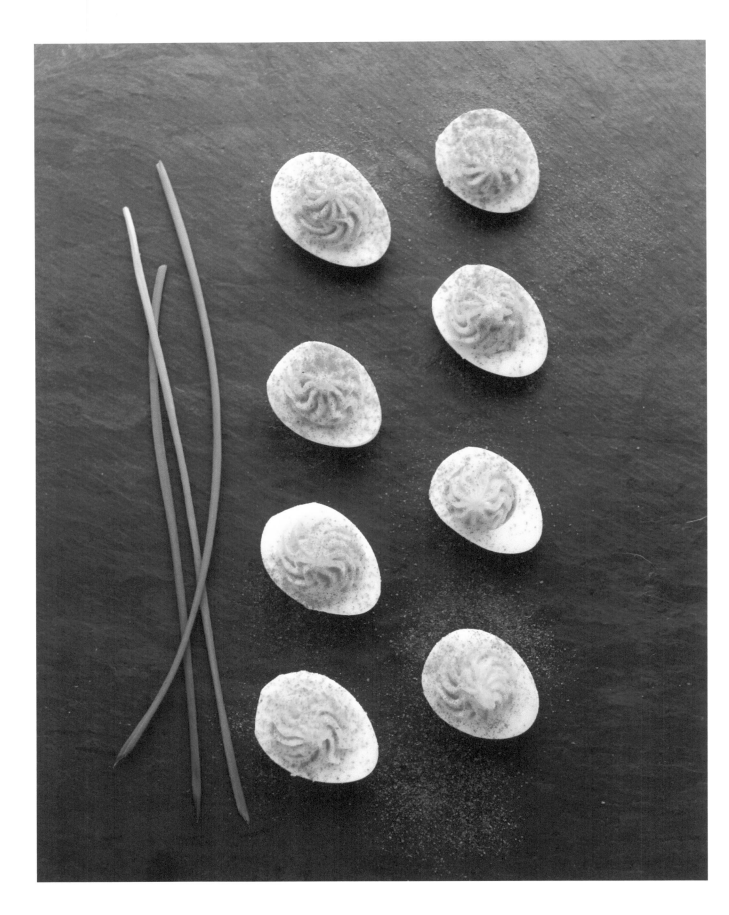

HORS D'OEUVRES

St. Maarten Meatballs
With Barbecue Sauce *14*
Parmesan Toasts *15*
Smoked Salmon Rosettes
With Honey Mustard *16*
Deviled Quail Eggs *17*
Steamed Baby Artichokes *20*
Seafood With Aioli *21*

ST. MAARTEN MEATBALLS WITH BARBECUE SAUCE

I JOINED THE "VIP Passenger" club at the St. Maarten airport mostly because of the meatball hors d'oeuvres they served. Travelers line up to get them and are disappointed if their flight leaves before the meatballs are ready. After great effort, I was able to persuade the club to share the recipe. Warning: Make the meatballs small enough that everyone will not get too full before dinner. If you want to make more of meatballs, though, I offer other recipes in the Appetizer and Poultry chapters. Minced meat is simply so versatile.

Makes 30 to 40 hors d'oeuvres

Sauce
¾ cup ketchup
½ cup Kraft Basic barbecue sauce
½ cup honey
3 cloves garlic, finely chopped
2 Tbsp. crushed red pepper
1½ tsp. hot pepper sauce
½ tsp. ground cinnamon
¼ tsp. celery salt

Meatballs
½ lb. (227 g) ground beef
½ lb. (227 g) ground pork
½ cup finely chopped onion
¼ cup finely chopped celery
Salt and pepper, to taste
¼ cup canola oil

Sauce
Combine all ingredients in Dutch oven or large deep skillet. Bring to boil. Reduce heat; simmer 15 min. Meanwhile, prepare Meatballs.

Meatballs
Mix all ingredients except oil just until blended; shape into 1-inch meatballs. Heat oil in large skillet. Add meatballs; cook until evenly browned, turning occasionally.

Add Meatballs to Sauce; simmer 15 min. or until meatballs are done (160°F), stirring occasionally. Transfer to serving dish. Serve with toothpicks.

TIP
• For best results, use freshly ground well-trimmed beef and pork from your butcher.

PARMESAN TOASTS

CESAR SOLA, a longtime friend, shared this recipe with me years ago, and it continues to be a great hit. The cheese topping can be made in advance and spread onto the bread slices; just cut into shapes and refrigerate until you're ready to bake them. When you cook these, you have to watch carefully to be sure they just get golden-brown and don't burn. Use the thin-sliced Pepperidge Farm bread or cut pitas to make rounds or squares for best results.

Makes 16 to 20 appetizers

1 cup grated Parmesan cheese
1/3 cup mayonnaise
2 Tbsp. grated red onion
4 thin slices white or whole wheat bread

Heat oven to 400°F.

Mix cheese, mayonnaise and onions; spread onto bread slices.

Use 1- to 1½-inch cookie cutter to cut bread into rounds or squares; place in single layer on baking sheet.

Bake 12 min. or until golden brown. Serve warm.

TIPS
•*When preparing the cheese mixture, add just enough mayonnaise to bind the ingredients together.*

• *Cheese mixture can be spread onto bread slices ahead of time. Cut into shapes, then refrigerate until ready to bake as directed just before serving.*

SMOKED SALMON WITH HONEY MUSTARD

THE PRESENTATION is especially important in the success of these hors d'oeuvres, which always do well, but if I were to describe how to make the rosettes we'd be here till Christmas. The idea of using honey mustard with smoked salmon I got from my brother and sister-in-law's chef, Ricky Soares.

Makes about 2 dozen hors d'oeuvres

6 slices pumpernickel bread, lightly toasted
Honey Cup Honey Mustard
½ lb. (227 g) smoked salmon, thinly sliced
Chopped fresh dill or chives (for garnish)

Spread toast slices lightly with honey mustard.

Cut into 1-inch rounds with cookie cutter.

Cut salmon into 3x1-inch strips; roll into rosettes or any other shapes to thoroughly cover rounds. Place on toast rounds.

Garnish with dill or chives.

TIP
• Toast bread slices in toaster. Or, place on baking sheet and toast in 300°F oven 3 to 4 min. or until lightly toasted on both sides, turning halfway through the baking time.

DEVILED QUAIL EGGS

QUAIL EGGS ARE JUST the right size for hors d'oeuvres. Filling them with a mixture of curry, mango chutney, balsamic vinegar and mayonnaise makes them even better. I mix the filling early; if it's not strong enough I add more of the chutney. The eggs look tired fast, so pipe the filling in right before the guests arrive. If you're going to use a pastry bag — which is the only way to fill these — you have to chop the chutney to make sure it fits through the tip. Using more curry powder as a garnish amplifies the flavor. You do need to add a few chicken eggs here because you will need more yolk than quail eggs will give you.

Recipe continues on page 18

Recipe continued from page 17

Makes 60 hors d'oeuvres

30 quail eggs
3 large chicken eggs
¼ cup mayonnaise, preferably Lesieur
1 Tbsp. curry powder,
    plus more for garnish if desired
1 tsp. balsamic vinegar
¼ tsp. salt
¼ cup finely chopped Major Grey's
    mango chutney (or more)
Paprika for garnish

Steam quail eggs 7 min. and steam chicken eggs 13 min. Crack open one of each to be sure they're cooked through before removing the rest. Immediately transfer steamed eggs to bowl of cold water and lightly crack the shells. Let stand 5 min. or until eggs are cool enough to handle.

Peel eggs; cut lengthwise in half. Carefully remove yolks; reserve whites. Place yolks in coarse strainer placed on top of bowl. Use wooden spoon to press yolks through strainer. Mix mayonnaise, curry powder, balsamic vinegar and salt in a small bowl. Blend into the yolks. Add enough of the chutney to moisten egg yolk mixture to desired consistency (the filling should not be too wet or it will be difficult to pipe). Mix well.

Spoon yolk mixture into pastry bag fitted with star tip. Use to pipe yolk mixture into quail egg white halves (if you have any left over, pipe it into one or two of the reserved chicken egg whites). Garnish with paprika, or with curry powder for more flavor. Refrigerate until chilled before serving.

TIPS

• *When peeling the eggs, take one quail egg out after six to seven minutes to test for doneness and one chicken egg out after 12 or 13. Also move eggs around so the whites are evenly distributed. (Yolks are of course heavier than whites.) Peel them under cold running water.*

• *Use the Ateco #864 star tip for the pastry bag, or another similar tip.*

STEAMED BABY ARTICHOKES

THE IMPORTANT THING here is the purchasing. Buy very small artichokes, of similar size if possible. They should be green and not look old or tired. Then you have to peel off all the outer leaves to get to the tender center. You can steam artichoke hearts with just water, but if you use chicken or vegetable broth they will pick up flavor. You can take them to another level by deep-frying them after they are steamed. These are good with plain vinaigrette but better with Herb Vinaigrette (page 58).

Baby artichokes
Chicken or vegetable stock or broth,
  purchased or homemade, or water
Vegetable oil, if frying
Herb Vinaigrette

Remove and discard dark outer leaves from artichokes. Use vegetable peeler to peel imperfections off bottoms of artichokes.

Cut artichokes lengthwise in half. Add to steamer basket placed over saucepan of simmering broth; steam just until tender.

Serve warm.

Or, if desired, deep-fry steamed artichokes. Heat oil to 350°F. Drain artichokes well; pat dry. Add, in batches if necessary, to hot oil; fry 1 min. or until crisp. Remove from oil with slotted spoon; drain on paper towels. Serve with Herb Vinaigrette.

SEAFOOD WITH AIOLI

PROVENCAL AIOLI has always been a favorite, and this particular recipe with good cold shellfish is unique. You can also add diced avocado to the seafood mixture, serve the mixture in avocado halves or, best of all, present it alongside stripes of Avocado Accent (page 42).

Makes ½ cup sauce

2 tsp. saffron threads,
  finely chopped or crushed into small pieces
½ cup mayonnaise
~~*1 garlic clove, minced, mashed*~~ ¼ tsp. minced garlic
1 to 2 tsp. harissa or 3 to 4 tsp.
  Hot Red Calabrian Pepper Jelly
Salt and pepper, to taste
Cooked seafood (shrimp or cut-up lobster)
Small toast rounds, Tostito Scoops
  or Siljan Croustades ★
Finely chopped chives, for garnish

Toast saffron in a small saucepan over low heat 30 to 60 seconds or until fragrant and lightly toasted, shaking pan constantly to prevent saffron from burning.

Whisk mayonnaise, garlic and harissa or jelly until blended. (Adjust any ingredients to suit your taste. Stir in saffron and add salt and pepper to taste. Toss seafood with enough aioli to coat. Spoon onto toast rounds or into Tostito Scoops or croustades. Garnish with chives.

★ Siljan Croustades are carried in upscale cheese or specialty markets or can be ordered from Amazon.

APPETIZERS

Crabmeat With Thai
Sweet Red Chile Sauce *24*
Shrimp and Avocado *25*
Tuna Tartare With Sushi Rice,
Fried Plantains and Avocado Accent *26*
Duck Spring Rolls *29*
Marinated Duck Confit *32*
Lentil Salad *34*
Gravlax With Scandia Sauce *35*
Beef Meatballs *38*

CRABMEAT WITH THAI SWEET RED CHILE SAUCE

I'M A GREAT FAN of Thai sweet chile sauce; I first had crabmeat served with it at Tamarind restaurant in St. Bart's. Making this with good Lesieur mayonnaise gives a very special taste. The plantain chips — which you can either make from scratch or buy — are a great complement (if gluten matters) because they are not made with white flour.

Makes 4 servings

1 lb. (454 g) cooked lump crabmeat
  (extra jumbo, if available)
½ cup Thai sweet red chile sauce
2 Tbsp. chopped fresh chives
2 Tbsp. mayonnaise
1/8 tsp. black peppercorns, coarsely ground
Pinch of kosher salt
½ Tbsp. chopped fresh chives (for garnish)
12 to 25 plantain chips or potato chips,
  depending on size

Remove and discard any pieces of cartilage from crabmeat, being careful not to break the lumps of crabmeat into smaller pieces. Place crabmeat in small bowl. In a separate bowl, mix together chili sauce, chives, mayonnaise, ground peppercorns and salt. Add to crab; mix lightly. Refrigerate several hours or until chilled.

To serve, use a spoon to divide the crab mixture among 4 salad plates. Garnish with chives. Serve with chips.

Note: This crab mix is also good presented with frisée and stripes of Avocado Accent, from the Sauces chapter.

TIP
• *I prefer Inka Sweet Plantain Chips. Call 1-800-808-0858 for assistance in finding where you can purchase them.*

SHRIMP AND AVOCADO WITH COCKTAIL SAUCE

SHRIMP AND AVOCADO combined with cocktail sauce is always a hit, although this is also very good with Mayo-Chile sauce (page 44). The sauce here can be made up to three days in advance. You can also substitute crab or lobster for the shrimp.

Makes 4 servings

Cocktail Sauce
½ cup mayonnaise
1/3 cup plus 1 Tbsp. ketchup
1 Tbsp. thinly sliced fresh chives
1 Tbsp. red wine vinegar
2 tsp. grated red onion
Salt and pepper, to taste
1 lb. (454 g) cleaned and steamed extra-large shrimp (16 to 20 count)
1½ Tbsp. thinly sliced fresh chives for garnish

Avocado Accent (page 42)

Sauce
Whisk all ingredients until blended.

Assembly
Cut each shrimp diagonally into 3 or 4 pieces; place in medium bowl. Add Cocktail Sauce. Toss to evenly coat. Set aside.

Cut 4 rounds of parchment paper slightly wider than 3-x 1½-inch metal collars. Place on sheet pan and top with collars. Spoon Avocado Accent into collars. Arrange shrimp over avocado base. Place in freezer for 20 to 30 minutes to set, then reserve in refrigerator until needed.

To serve, peel off parchment. Place each portion on a small serving plate and remove collar. Sprinkle with chives. (Alternatively, you can lay out the shrimp in strips alternating with the Avocado Accent.)

TUNA TARTARE WITH AVOCADO ACCENT

THE FIRST THING you need for a good tartare is great tuna. Basically you have to be willing to scrap the part of the tuna with all the unpleasant sinews in it (If you scrape the tuna off the sinews with a spoon, though, you can use that part for another dish.). You can keep tuna for several days in the refrigerator, however its color will change after a day or two. When you cut the pieces, you want a very small dice but not to the point of mush; there should still be texture. Putting it through large holes on the meat grinder on a Cuisinart works well. You also want to add the sauce slowly so that it gives enough taste but doesn't get too liquid. Finally, chives do not change the taste much but do add a great deal to the appearance. You can also make this using salmon. If you're feeling ambitious, serve the tartare with the Sushi Rice and Fried Plantains that follow; otherwise just serve with plantain chips.

Makes 3 or 4 first-course servings

Tuna Tartare
2 Tbsp. Thai red chile sauce
1 tsp. soy sauce
1 tsp. lemon juice
1 tsp. sesame oil
¼ to ½ tsp. sriracha, or to taste
¼ tsp. salt
⅛ tsp. black pepper
1 Tbsp. thinly sliced fresh chives, divided
9oz. to 1lb. (454 g) fresh tuna, cut into small dice

Avocado Accent (page 42)

Tartare
Make a sauce with the chile sauce, soy sauce, lemon juice, sesame oil, sriracha, salt and pepper. Stir in half the chives.

Add enough sauce to tuna until of desired consistency; mix lightly. Refrigerate until chilled. Garnish with remaining chives.

To plate, arrange the tuna tartare in strips about the width of a tongue depressor in the center of each plate. Add one strip of Avocado Accent alongside.

Recipe continues on page 28

Recipe continued from page 26

Sushi Rice
1 cup sushi rice
1 cup water
100 grams rice vinegar
50 grams sugar
5 grams salt
Seaweed for garnish

Plantains
1 plantain
Lemon juice
Oil for deep-frying
Miel de Caña molasses
  (or regular light molasses)
Salt

Sushi Rice
Rinse rice three or four times. Place in pot with water and bring to a boil. Reduce to a simmer. Cook 20 minutes. Cover surface with plastic wrap and hold over low heat until the last water is absorbed, 5 to 10 minutes. Meanwhile, combine the vinegar, sugar and rice and mix well.

Spread out on a baking sheet. Pour the vinegar mixture over and mix well. Let stand 10 to 15 minutes to absorb the seasoning. Do not refrigerate. Shape into small balls.

Plantains
Peel both plantains. Using a mandoline, cut into 2-inch-long matchsticks. Place in lemon juice a few minutes, then drain.

Fry in 350-degree oil until golden brown. Drain on paper towels.

Heat molasses in pot and add plantains; heat until coated. Salt to taste. Serve in paper cones alongside tuna tartare and rice balls.

DUCK SPRING ROLLS

THIS RECIPE, which starts with purchased duck confit, was given to me by Jean Claude Dufour at Restaurant L'Esprit in St. Barts. It takes a little practice to roll the spring rolls correctly and then fry them right, but they are well worth the effort. An electric deep-fryer makes the cooking easier. These make a marvelous appetizer, teamed with either Asian Spring Roll Sauce (page 42) or Mayo-Chile Sauce (page 44).

Recipe continues on page 30

Recipe continued from page 29

Makes 8 to 10 servings

Filling
300 g duck confit
200 g butternut squash,
  peeled, seeded, julienned (2-inch strips)
110 g cooked vermicelli,
  cooled, cut into 2-inch lengths
20 g chopped fresh cilantro
20 g kimchi base
15 g rice vinegar
2 tsp. salt
2 tsp. ground pepper

Spring Rolls
1 egg yolk
½ tsp. water
8 to 10 egg roll wrappers (7½-inch square)
Vegetable oil, for frying
Asian Spring Roll Sauce or Mayo-Chile Sauce

Filling
Remove and discard skin, bones and sinew from confit. Shred meat; place in medium bowl. Add remaining ingredients; mix well. Adjust seasoning, if necessary.

Spring Rolls
Whisk egg yolk and water until blended. Place 1 egg roll wrapper on clean dry surface. Spoon about 60 g Filling slightly below center of wrapper. Fold corner of wrapper clos-est to filling over filling, tucking point of wrapper under filling. Roll up, folding in op-posite side corners as you roll spring roll up to completely enclose filling. Brush re-maining corner with egg wash, then press into spring roll to seal. Repeat with remaining wrappers and filling.

Heat oil in deep fryer to 350°F to 375°F. Add spring rolls, in batches; fry until crisp and golden brown. (Do not overcook.) Drain on paper towels. Serve with sauce.

TIPS
• *Any holes or large air pockets will allow oil to seep in, resulting in a greasy egg roll!*

• *Use a mandoline or the large holes on a box grater to easily cut the peeled squash into julienne strips, removing two layers of peel (until down to one color) before cutting the squash into strips.*

MARINATED DUCK CONFIT

MARINATING SHREDDED duck meat in vinegar and spicy oil transforms it for a frisée-and-mango salad, as described below. But I also like hiding a tablespoonful or so in the bottom of a bowl of a cold summer soup like gazpacho as a surprise. It is also excellent in Lentil Salad on the following page. The recipe was given to me by Giuliano Bugialli.

Makes 4 servings for salad,
more for hors d'oeuvres

1 to 2 duck legs in confit
1 Tbsp. sugar
1 Tbsp. salt
1 Tbsp. red wine vinegar
1 tsp. pepper
1 clove
Pinch of crushed red pepper
¾ cup olive oil, or more if necessary, to cover

Remove skin and fat from duck legs. Thickly shred meat into even pieces, about ⅛ inch by 1 inch. Place in glass bowl.

Combine all remaining ingredients; pour over duck. (If necessary add more oil if needed to completely cover duck with marinade.)

Let stand at room temperature 2 to 3 hours, then refrigerate until fat congeals and can be easily removed. Marinate several days. (The duck can be stored up to one week.)

Drain duck; discard marinade.

TIP
• *To make a salad for one person, combine duck with 2 cups bite-size frisée or other salad greens plus ⅓ cup each diced mango and quartered figs. Drizzle with Herb Vinaigrette (page 58).*

LENTIL SALAD

OF ALL THE PLACES that serve lentil salad in St. Barts, Taiwana used to have the most popular. But I must confess I find my version much more compelling. The balsamic vinegar coupled with the pancetta or chorizo puts it over the top, although you can substitute Marinated Duck Confit (page 34) for either of those.

Makes 4 servings

1 cup dried French green lentils
3 sprigs fresh thyme
3 garlic cloves, minced
1¼ qt. (5 cups) water, or more if necessary
2 or 3 slices cooked pancetta
    (about ¼ inch thick), medium dice,
    or Spanish chorizo in ⅛-inch dice
1½ Tbsp. Dijon mustard
3 Tbsp. aged balsamic vinegar
2 Tbsp. olive oil
Salt and pepper, to taste
2 Tbsp. minced fresh chives or parsley
    (for garnish)

Bring lentils, thyme, garlic and water to boil in large saucepan; simmer 25 min. or just until lentils start to soften, adding more water if necessary to keep lentils covered with water as they cook.

Drain lentils while still warm; remove and discard thyme sprigs. Place lentils in medium bowl. Add cooked pancetta or chorizo (or duck confit) and all remaining ingredients except chives; mix lightly.

Garnish with chives.

GRAVLAX WITH SCANDIA SAUCE

I TRIED THE GRAVLAX at Peter Grünaeur's new Austrian restaurant on the Upper East Side, Grünauer, and asked him to teach me the recipe. The juniper berries and gin bring it up a notch. The sauce comes from Maurice Moore Betty, who was my first cooking teacher. It's very good, although you can serve the salmon without it.

Recipe continues on page 36

Recipe continued from page 35

Makes 8 to 10 servings

Gravlax

1 fillet boneless, skinless Atlantic salmon,
  2½ to 3 pounds cut from the thick end
4 oz. gin
½ cup kosher salt
½ cup brown sugar
¼ cup ground black pepper
2 Tbsp. juniper berries
12 whole black peppercorns
1 bunch fresh dill, washed,
  with 1 Tbsp. reserved for the sauce

Sauce

1½ Tbsp. Lambrusco vinegar
1 Tbsp. Dijon mustard
1 tsp sugar
¼ tsp kosher salt
Dash white pepper
¼ cup canola oil
1 Tbsp. chopped fresh dill
1 tsp lemon juice

Gravlax

Place the salmon in a glass dish just large enough to hold it. Drizzle the gin evenly over. Sprinkle evenly with the salt, brown sugar, ground black pepper, juniper berries and peppercorns. Lay the fresh dill on top. Cover with plastic wrap and weight the fish down, making sure the weight is evenly distributed. Refrigerate for 3 days.

Sauce

Combine the vinegar, mustard, sugar, salt and white pepper in a bowl. Whisk in the olive oil. Add the dill and lemon juice and mix well.

To serve, remove the salmon from the marinade, brush or scrapew off the seasonings and pat dry. Slice against the grain into very thin slices, working the blade back and forth and letting the knife do the work. Serve with the sauce on top or on the side.

BEEF MEATBALLS

THERE ARE LOTS of meatball recipes, but I find this one particularly satisfying. I'm not sure where I got it, I just know it's a favorite. Two types of cheese plus prosciutto and basil make these unusual; they don't even need a sauce. If you want to serve them with pasta, add a tomato sauce.

Makes 20 to 30 meatballs

2 Tbsp. olive oil
1 small red onion, finely chopped
½ green pepper, finely chopped
2 lb. ground chuck
1 cup fresh or dry bread crumbs
1 cup grated Parmigiano-Reggiano
½ cup ricotta
6 oz. thinly sliced prosciutto, finely chopped
½ cup fresh basil, chopped
3 Tb sp. chopped fresh parsley
Dash hot pepper sauce
3 egg yolks
Salt and pepper, to taste
All-purpose flour, to dust
Vegetable oil, for frying

Heat olive oil in small skillet over medium heat. Add onions and green peppers; sauté 7 min. or until tender. Remove from heat.

Mix ground chuck, bread crumbs, Parmigiano, ricotta, prosciutto, basil, parsley and hot pepper sauce in large bowl just until blended. Add egg yolks, one at a time, mixing after each just until blended. Add cooked vegetables, mix lightly. Season with salt and black pepper.

Shape meat mixture into 2-inch balls. Roll, 1 at a time, in flour just until lightly coated.

Heat vegetable oil in large skillet over medium-high heat. Add meatballs, in batches; cook until evenly browned, turning occasionally. (Be careful to not burn the meatballs.) Partially cover the skillet; cook meatballs additional 10 to 12 min. or until done (160°F). Remove from skillet; cool.

Reine de Joie
Color lithograph • Henri de Toulouse-Lautrec, Paris 1892
Alfred Stieglitz Collection, 1949
THE METROPOLITAN MUSEUM OF ART • NEW YORK NY

Condiment Dish, Possibly Egypt, Syria, or Iraq, 8th or 9th century.
Earthenware, molded and glazed.
The Madina Collection of Islamic Art, gift of Camilla Chandler Frost.

SAUCES, CONDIMENTS AND SEASONINGS

AVOCADO ACCENT

I MADE UP the recipe for this rich avocado spread, which is very versatile. You can serve it in stripes alongside Seafood in Aioli, Crabmeat With Thai Sweet Chili Sauce or Tuna Tartare. It is also very good as the base of a shrimp or crabmeat cocktail.

Makes at least enough for 4 servings

2 fully ripe avocados, peeled, pitted
2 Tbsp. olive oil
2 Tbsp. fresh lemon juice
1½ Tbsp. finely chopped fresh cilantro
1½ Tbsp. finely chopped scallions
¼ tsp. salt
¼ tsp. sugar

Mash avocado in medium bowl with whisk.

Combine remaining ingredients; gradually add to avocado, mixing after each addition until you reach the right flavor and consistency. Serve immediately, reserving any remaining oil mixture for another use.

ASIAN SPRING ROLL SAUCE

MADE WITH SPICY kimchi base, this is an excellent accompaniment for anything from duck rolls to seared tuna. The recipe is from a favorite chef in St. Barts, Jean Claude Dufour of Restaurant L'Esprit. It works best when made with an immersion blender.

Makes 6 to 8 servings

1 large egg
2 cups grapeseed oil
¼ cup water
3 Tbsp. kimchi base, or to taste
Salt and pepper, to taste
Juice from ½ to 1 lime

Blend all ingredients except lime juice in bowl with immersion blender.

Add lime juice to taste and blend again.

BEST PESTO

THIS COMES FROM a small restaurant in Siena whose name is less memorable to me than the flavor. What's special about this version is that it contains both pine nuts and walnuts and both Parmigiano-Reggiano and pecorino, which give a more intense taste. It's even better if you use an old-fashioned nut grinder — I have one I bought at a flea market some years ago. Try this sauce either with pasta as usual or over sliced garden-fresh or roasted tomatoes.

Makes enough for 4 pasta portions

3 oz. (80 g) pine nuts
1½ oz. (40 g) walnuts
1½ tsp. coarse salt
100 g small fresh basil leaves
3 garlic cloves, quartered
70 g grated Parmigiano-Reggiano
30 g grated Pecorino Romano
2 Tbsp. olive oil
2 Tbsp. hot water

Process pine nuts, nuts and salt in food processor until nuts are finely ground. Add basil and garlic; pulse just until incorporated.

Add cheeses. Gradually add oil, then hot water through feed tube at top of processor while processing with pulsing action until smooth.

If serving with pasta, heat the prepared pesto in large saucepan a few minutes before the pasta is done. Drain pasta, reserving about a cup of the cooking water. Add about 6 Tbsp.

of the reserved pasta cooking water to pesto; mix well. Add pasta; stir to evenly coat. If it's too dry, add more water. Plate pasta; sprinkle with additional ½ cup Parmigiano Reggiano. Garnish with basil chiffonade.

TIP
• *Wash the fresh basil leaves carefully, then dry them in a salad spinner. Or, gently pat them dry with paper towels or clean kitchen towel.*

PUMMAROLA/TOMATO SAUCE

I LEARNED THIS SPECIAL pomodoro sauce from Giuliano Bugialli around 2004, when he was helping me develop recipes for an upscaled restaurant at Bergdorf Goodman. It's unique because you basically steam the tomatoes and vegetables for an hour and a half while they get very sweet.

Makes 2 to 3 cups

2 28-oz. cans crushed tomatoes
¼ cup chopped red onion
1 celery stalk, chopped
1 carrot, chopped
1 large garlic clove, minced
2 Tbsp. olive oil
10 fresh parsley sprigs, large stems removed
8 large fresh basil leaves
2 Tbsp. butter
Salt and pepper, to taste

Recipe continues on page 44

Recipe continued from page 43

Combine all ingredients except butter and salt and pepper in large saucepan. Bring to a simmer; cover. Simmer over low heat 1½ hours, uncovering and gently shaking pan every 10 to 15 min. to prevent ingredients from sticking to bottom of pan. Vegetables should be very soft.

Press sauce through a food mill fitted with either a fine or medium disk. Return to pan. Add butter; cook until butter is melted and sauce is reduced to desired consistency, stirring frequently. Season with salt and pepper.

MAYO-CHILE SAUCE

THIS IS BETTER than cocktail sauce with shrimp, lobster or crab. Using both Thai sweet chile sauce and sriracha gives it a particular kick; Lesieur mayonnaise, from France, also makes a big difference. The recipe came from the chef at the Rye Bar and Southern Kitchen at the Marriott in Raleigh, N.C.

Makes 1 ³/₄ cups

1 cup mayonnaise
½ cup Thai sweet chile sauce
1 Tbsp. lemon juice
Salt and pepper, to taste
1 to 2 Tbsp. sriracha
Chopped chives for garnish

Mix all ingredients except sriracha until blended.

Add 1 Tbsp. of the sriracha; mix well.

If desired, stir in remaining sriracha to taste. Garnish with chives.

DARK STOCK AND RED WINE SAUCE

DANNY BROWN OF X BAR on the Upper East Side of Manhattan shared this recipe. The combination of very rich stock and dry red wine, both reduced for maximum flavor, results in an intense sauce. Try it with any steak off the grill, however it's also marvelous for steak when you can't charcoal-grill.

Makes 3 cups, enough for 12 servings

Dark Stock
15 pounds chicken bones (backs, wings, necks)
  or a combination of chicken and other bones*
1 very large carrot, coarsely chopped
1 celery stalk, coarsely chopped
2 large Spanish onions, coarsely chopped
2 heads garlic, outer skins removed
  but cloves not peeled
2 Tbsp. tomato paste
5 sprigs fresh thyme
7 sprigs fresh parsley
2 bay leaves

Red Wine Reduction
1 750ml bottle red wine
1 cup port
¼ cup chopped shallots
¼ cup peeled and lightly bruised garlic cloves
¼ cup chopped carrot

Stock
Heat the oven to 400 degrees. Oil the bones and spread onto sheet pans. Roast until deep golden brown. Remove from the sheet pans and reserve. Drain off the fat. Using a spatula, scrape the drippings from the pans into a large stockpot. Add the drained bones and the remaining ingredient. Add water to cover and bring to a boil. Reduce heat and simmer 5 to 6 hours, adding water as needed to keep the bones covered.

Discard bones and strain stock into storage containers. Refrigerate until fat can be removed from the surface (save for other uses). Return the stock to the pot and cook until reduced by 70 to 80 percent, or until it is very thick. You should have about 3 cups.

If you are not making the sauce right away, the stock can be refrigerated for 1 week or frozen for a year or so.

Red Wine Reduction
Combine all ingredients in a saucepan and cook until reduced to ½ cup.

Sauce
Combine Stock and Red Wine Reduction and cook until reduced to a sauce consistency. Serve.

* If making a sauce for veal, lamb or beef, you may add bones from those meats. If you choose to use veal bones, be sure to start by blanching them and then shocking them in cold water before browning them.

TIPS
• Do not use bones from kosher chickens or the stock will be too salty.

• Necks make the best chicken stock, but they are hard to find. Fleischer's at 1325 Third Avenue in New York City carries them (646 880 6688).

• Ridged sheet pans work best for browning the bones. You can find them at Sur La Table.

APPLE CURRY SAUCE

THIS IS A COMPOSITE of various curry sauces I have come across over the years. The apple and the orange juice add sweetness, the coconut milk richness and flavor. It's very good with shrimp or other seafood, or with chicken.

Makes about 2 to 3 servings

1 tablespoon butter
1 tablespoon olive oil
100 grams (about 3½ ounces) onion,
    finely chopped
135 grams (about 5 ounces) apple,
    peeled and finely chopped
1 garlic clove, finely chopped
1 cup orange juice
½ to ¾ cup heavy cream
¼ cup coconut milk
1 Tbsp. curry powder

In a medium pot, heat butter and olive oil. Add onion and sauté until translucent, about 3 to 5 minutes. Add apple and cook until slightly softened. Add garlic and orange juice and cook until liquid is reduced by 80 percent. Add heavy cream to taste, coconut milk and curry power and cook 3 to 5 minutes more, until liquid starts to thicken. Season with salt and pepper. Add more curry powder if you like.

BLACKENING MIX

I USE THIS SPICE combination mostly on tuna. If you cook tuna in a frying pan it's very difficult to achieve a seared look, and the fish itself can be relatively tasteless. This spicy blend, which was given to me by my friend Barbara Wyatt, gives marvelous color and taste to tuna. You can make it well in advance and also use it in other dishes.

Makes about ½ cup

2 Tbsp. (½ oz.) paprika
2 Tbsp. (½ oz.) chili powder
1 Tbsp. plus 1 tsp. (½ oz.) salt
2 tsp. ground cumin
2 tsp. sugar
1 tsp. dry mustard
1 tsp. black pepper
1 tsp. dried thyme leaves
1 tsp. dried oregano leaves
1 tsp. curry powder
½ tsp. cayenne

Mix all ingredients until blended.

Store in airtight container at room temperature up to several months before using as desired.

ONION CONFIT

IF YOU'RE HAVING a hamburger or steak and want a tasty accompaniment, onion confit does the trick. Red wine and sherry vinegar add acidity, and grenadine enhances the sweetness of the onions. For best results, cool slightly or to room temperature before using.

Makes 4 to 6 condiment side servings

1 cup butter
3 lb. yellow onions, thinly sliced
2¼ cups robust red wine
¼ cup sherry vinegar
¼ cup grenadine
3 Tbsp. brown sugar
1 Tbsp. plus 1 tsp. (16 g) salt
2 tsp. (10 g) black pepper

Melt butter in large heavy-bottomed skillet. Add ⅓ of the onions; sauté until onions start to soften, then add remaining onions in two separate batches. Cook until onions are translucent, stirring constantly to avoid burning.

Add wine and vinegar; cook until reduced by half, stirring frequently. Stir in remaining ingredients; cook until most the liquid is cooked off, stirring constantly.

TOMATO KETCHUP

THIS HOMEMADE ketchup is a variation on a recipe given to me by my friend Donald Zilka. Ancho chilies add a little heat.

Makes about 1 quart

2 qt. small ripe tomatoes, roughly chopped
2 cups red wine vinegar
⅔ cup packed dark brown sugar
3 small dried ancho chiles, seeded, minced
1 Tbsp. kosher salt
1 Tbsp. ground black pepper
1 Tbsp. maple syrup

Bring all ingredients except syrup to boil in large saucepan. Reduce heat to medium-low; simmer 35 to 45 min. or until reduced to thick jam-like consistency, sitting occasionally.

Pour into food processor; process until smooth. Strain through a fine mesh metal sieve. Return strained mixture to saucepan. Stir in maple syrup; bring just to a simmer. Remove from heat; cool completely. Refrigerate up to 1 week before serving.

MUSTARD SAUCE FOR COLD SEAFOOD

THIS IS A GOOD, pungent alternative to the usual cocktail sauce. It's especially good with the mussels left from the Scallops recipes in the Seafood chapter (pages 94 and 109).

Makes about 1 cup

1 cup mayonnaise, preferable Lesieur
1 Tbsp. plus 1 tsp. Colman's mustard
2 tsp. Worcestershire sauce
1 tsp. A-1 steak sauce
2 Tbsp. heavy cream
Salt and freshly ground black pepper
1 Tbsp. chopped fresh chives

Combine mayonnaise and mustard in small bowl and mix well. Blend in remaining ingredients.

SALADS AND DRESSINGS

GOTHAM SALAD

THIS WAS INSPIRED by a salad served at the Polo Lounge at the Beverly Hills Hotel called the Neil McCarthy Salad, named for a 1940s polo-playing Hollywood lawyer who was very specific about the proteins he wanted with his greens. I was so fond of it I would dissect it in my hotel room to try to get the recipe right for a chopped salad I wanted to serve in my restaurant at Bergdorf Goodman some time ago. It became — and from what I hear still is — the most popular salad there. The Bergdorf people put out a cookbook that features the Gotham Salad; however it fails to give me credit. My solace is that I'm still giving credit to the Neil McCarthy Salad of the Beverly Hills Hotel. You can also add a quarter of an avocado, diced and fanned out around the salad.

Makes 1 salad

2 cups very finely chopped iceberg lettuce
1 ounce hard-cooked egg yolk, chopped
1 ounce hard-cooked egg white, chopped
1/3 cup cooked chicken breast
    cut into 1/4-inch cubes
1/3 cup ham cut into 1/4-inch cubes
1/3 cup Gruyere or Cheddar
    cut into 1/4-inch cubes
1 ounce tomato cut into small dice
1/3 cup red beets cut into small dice
3 sprigs watercress
1 ounce crispy cooked bacon
2 to 4 tablespoons Gotham Salad Dressing
    (page 59) or Russian Dressing (page 57),
    or to taste
Salt and freshly ground black pepper to taste

Mound lettuce in center of plate.
Toss egg yolk and white together to combine. Alternating light- and dark-colored ingredients, arrange everything but the dressing, watercress and bacon either in a triangle or in rows on top of the lettuce. Carefully place watercress sprigs in the center of the mound and crumble the bacon over the top. Serve with dressing on the side. Season with salt and pepper.

CAESAR SALAD

PIETRO'S, a very expensive Italian/steak restaurant on East 43rd Street, has one of the best steaks in New York, but the thing people come for, from far and wide, is the Caesar salad. Nobody gives out the recipe, but they have no quarrel if you go over to the table where the waiter is making it and take copious notes. Which is how I have been making this for many years (the restaurant has been around since 1932 but moved in the 1950s from the walkup on Third Avenue where my family went). The anchovies, the garlic and the Worcestershire are essential, but the most important part is my trick with the croutons. I do them by cutting white bread into cubes and sautéing them in lots of butter until they get golden brown, then putting them in a Ziploc bag with chopped rosemary, salt and pepper and shaking the bag.
The croutons go in wet and buttery and just drink up the intensity of the seasonings.

Makes 1 serving as a main course, 2 as a starter

1 Tbsp. coarsely chopped anchovies
1 tsp. minced garlic
1 egg yolk
½ tsp. Colman's dry mustard
2 tsp. Worcestershire sauce
2 Tbsp. Lambrusco vinegar or red wine vinegar
3 to 4 Tbsp. olive oil
Freshly ground black pepper to taste
4 to 5 loosely packed cups Romaine hearts
  cut crosswise into thin ribbons
½ cup Croutons (recipe follows)
6 to 8 Tbsp. grated Parmigiano-Reggiano

Place anchovies and garlic in medium salad bowl. Add egg yolk and whisk well. Add mustard, Worcestershire sauce and vinegar and whisk energetically until the mixture is thickened. Gradually whisk in the oil, adding enough to make a thick, creamy dressing. Season with freshly ground black pepper.

Add lettuce and croutons to bowl and mix lightly. Top with Parmigiano-Reggiano.

Croutons: Melt 1 to 2 Tbsp. butter with 1 Tbsp. olive oil in sauté pan over medium heat. When foam subsides, add ½ cup bread cubes (½ inch); cook until golden brown, stirring occasionally. Cool. Place bread cubes in resealable plastic bag. Add 1 tsp. salt and ½ tsp. ground black pepper; shake gently to evenly coat bread cubes. Store at room temperature until ready to use.

COLESLAW

THIS IS FROM a restaurant in Southampton called John Duck's, which was very popular for many years with both locals and summer visitors. Roast Long Island duck was a favorite there, but strangely enough one of the things that earned the greatest applause was the coleslaw, which The New York Times said "elevated the humble cabbage to legendary heights." Mark Westerhoff, the chef and co-owner with his brother, was working as a butcher at Citarella after the restaurant closed in 2008 and was kind enough to share the recipe with me.

Makes 6 to 8 servings

1½ lb. (700 g) white cabbage
7 oz. (120 g) carrots
7 oz. (120 g) celery
2 oz. (40 g) green pepper
2 oz. (40 g) onion
1¼ cups mayonnaise
3 Tbsp. sugar
2 tsp. celery salt
2 tsp. black pepper

Use food processor, mandolin or box grater to shred cabbage and vegetables; place in large bowl.

Mix remaining ingredients until blended. Add to cabbage mixture; toss to evenly coat.

Refrigerate several hours or until chilled.

COLESLAW, COUNTRY-STYLE

THIS IS ALSO a marvelous coleslaw, inspired by one they serve at Hillstone, East Hampton Grill and Palm Beach Grill and some 50 other restaurants with the same owner (Houston's is also part of the group). I'm not sure it's an exact replica, but I was assisted by a past chef at Hillstone in developing it, so I think it's close. Two types of cabbage, hand-cut into chiffonade, are dressed with both mayonnaise and sour cream, with plenty of seasonings.

Makes 6 to 8 servings

4 cups hand-shredded green cabbage
  (¹/₈-inch chiffonade)
4 cups hand-shredded savoy cabbage
  (¹/₈-inch chiffonade)
2 scallions, white parts coarsely chopped
2 Tbsp. chopped fresh parsley
½ cup mayonnaise
2 Tbsp. sour cream
2 Tbsp. Champagne vinegar
2 tsp. yellow mustard
1 tsp. sugar
½ tsp. Spanish paprika
½ tsp. Colman's dry mustard
¼ tsp. garlic salt
¹/₈ tsp. black pepper

Combine cabbage, scallions and parsley in large bowl.

Whisk remaining ingredients in separate bowl until blended. Add to cabbage mixture; toss to evenly coat.

TIP
• *This easy-to-make coleslaw can be prepared ahead of time. Refrigerate up to 3 days before serving.*

CELERY ROOT REMOULADE

WE SERVED celery root remoulade as a side salad in the Bergdorf Goodman restaurants when I ran them for 27 years. This is the recipe I developed, which always had a great following. Using both Dijon and whole-grain mustard doubles the pungency. Make this well in advance to tenderize the celery root (which is often sold as celeriac).

Makes 4 to 6 servings

6 cups julienned peeled celery root
Lemon juice
½ cup mayonnaise
⅓ cup minced fresh parsley
1 Tbsp. plus 1 tsp. Dijon mustard
1 tsp. grainy mustard
Salt and pepper, to taste

Combine all ingredients in a medium bowl and mix lightly.

TIPS
• *Use large grating blade of food processor instead of hand grater to process the celery just until julienned. Be careful to not overprocess until puréed.*

• *Celery root can be julienned ahead of time. If preparing more than 2 hours before serving, toss with 2 tsp. lemon juice, then refrigerate until ready to use.*

EGG SALAD WITH TARRAGON, PARSLEY, MINT AND CHIVES

THIS IS ANOTHER salad we used to serve in the restaurants at Bergdorf Goodman.

Makes 3 to 4 servings

1 small shallot, diced
Few drops tarragon vinegar
*   or white wine vinegar*
6 eggs, hard cooked
3 Tbsp. mayonnaise
1 Tbsp. finely chopped fresh tarragon leaves
1 Tbsp. finely chopped fresh parsley
1 Tbsp. finely chopped fresh mint
1 Tbsp. finely chopped fresh chives
¼ tsp. sea salt
Freshly ground black pepper
Fresh chives (for garnish)

Place shallot in small bowl. Add vinegar; stir to evenly moisten. Let stand 5 min.

Meanwhile, chop eggs; place in medium bowl. Add all remaining ingredients except chive garnish; mix well.

Stir shallot mixture into egg mixture; spoon into serving bowl. Garnish with chives.

TIPS
• *If you used more than just a few drops of vinegar, drain the shallot before stirring it into the egg salad.*

• *Add more salt to taste, if desired.*

ALL-SEASON TOMATO SALAD

IN THE BERGDORF GOODMAN restaurants, people just expected to see tomatoes on the menu. But of course those don't taste very special except in late July and August in this part of the country. Marinating them turned out to be a great help in extending tomato season. The salt here looks excessive, but it almost cures the tomatoes. And the marinade is drained off before serving anyway. This is also great served with burrata.

Makes 2 to 4 servings

4 firm tomatoes (4½ oz. each)
1 Tbsp. salt
1 tsp. freshly ground black pepper
¼ cup red wine vinegar, preferably Lambrusco
5 Tbsp. olive oil, divided use
1 Tbsp. chopped fresh parsley or chives

Cut each tomato into 8 wedges; place in large bowl.

Add salt, pepper, vinegar and 2 Tbsp. oil; mix lightly. Let stand 2 hours.

Drain tomatoes just before serving; discard drained liquid.

Add parsley and remaining oil to tomatoes; mix lightly.

DIJON VINAIGRETTE

THIS RECIPE CAME from Pierre Mondard, and I think it's the dressing that Lenôtre in Paris uses. Two things make it special. The first is the Lambrusco vinegar, which I added instead of regular red wine vinegar. And the second is the hot water, which eliminates the sharp acidity. You can keep this in the refrigerator for at least a week.

Makes about ¾ cup

2 Tbsp. Dijon mustard
3 Tbsp. Lambrusco vinegar or red wine vinegar
3 Tbsp. olive oil
3 Tbsp. canola oil
2 to 3 Tbsp. hot water
Salt and black pepper, to taste

Whisk mustard and vinegar in medium bowl until blended. Slowly add olive oil, then canola oil, whisking after each addition until well blended.

Add enough hot water until the vinaigrette tastes like it has the proper acidity. Season with salt and pepper; whisk until blended.

ROQUEFORT CHEESE DRESSING

YEARS AGO, when I was building an industrial park at Brainard Field in Hartford, Connecticut, there was a restaurant called Hal's where we used to go eat lunch and they would make salad with this dressing at the table. The Worcestershire sauce makes it unusual.

Makes 1¼ cups

6 oz. Society Bee or other good-quality
   Roquefort cheese, crumbled
¼ cup Worcestershire sauce
2 Tbsp. Lambrusco vinegar or red wine vinegar
½ cup canola oil
Salt and pepper, to taste

Combine cheese, Worcestershire sauce and vinegar in medium bowl.

Slowly add oil, whisking after each addition until well blended.

Season with salt and pepper.

RUSSIAN DRESSING

RUSSIAN DRESSING is a component of a lot of my recipes. It's so much better when you make it yourself; as always, the Lesieur mayonnaise and Lambrusco vinegar make a big difference.

Makes about 1½ cups

1 cup mayonnaise, preferably Lesieur
½ cup ketchup
¼ cup drained pickle relish
2 Tbsp. Lambrusco vinegar or red wine vinegar
1 Tbsp. grated or minced red onion
½ to 1 tsp. sriracha
Salt and freshly ground black pepper, to taste

Mix ingredients until blended.

TIP
• *The prepared dressing can be stored in the refrigerator up to 1 week before serving.*

TARRAGON MAYONNAISE WITH ORANGE ZEST

THIS IS GOOD on chicken or lobster salad or on leafy greens. Tarragon always seems like a magic herb, and the orange zest gives it a little lift. You can start with supermarket mayonnaise, but I much prefer the French brand Lesieur instead, which I bring home in my suitcase but you can order from Amazon.

Makes about ¾ cup

½ cup mayonnaise
⅓ cup or more finely chopped
  fresh tarragon leaves
Leaves from several sprigs of fresh parsley,
  finely chopped
Zest from 1 small orange
Freshly ground white pepper
Salt, to taste

Mix all ingredients until blended.

HERB VINAIGRETTE

I GOT THIS RECIPE from Cuquita (Coketa) Arias when she was the chef at the Bristol Hotel in Panama. I find it's particularly good with steamed baby artichokes as it has a more interesting texture than regular Dijon vinaigrette. It's also excellent with jumbo lump crabmeat, shrimp or lobster. If you're using the seafood in a salad, frisee works best as the greens.

Makes enough for 8 (¾-cup) portions
of seafood or salad

2 Tbsp. Dijon mustard
3 Tbsp. red wine vinegar
3 Tbsp. sherry vinegar or Lambrusco vinegar
½ cup olive oil
½ cup canola oil
¼ cup honey
¼ cup finely chopped scallions
¼ cup plus 1 Tbsp. finely chopped fresh cilantro,
  divided use
¼ cup plus 1 Tbsp. finely chopped fresh parsley,
  divided use
Cooked jumbo crabmeat, medallions of lobster
  or shrimp

Whisk mustard and both vinegars in medium bowl until blended. Gradually add both oils, whisking after each addition until well blended. Stir in honey, scallions, honey, and ¼ cup each cilantro and parsley.

Spoon *⅓* cup sauce onto each of 8 serving plates; top with ¾ cup seafood. Sprinkle with remaining cilantro and parsley.

GOTHAM SALAD DRESSING

THIS IS THE DRESSING I developed for the Gotham Salad I served at my restaurants in Bergdorf Goodman. I've updated it with shallot instead of onion and more sophisticated flavorings in the chile sauce and relish.

Makes 1¾ cups

1 tablespoon minced shallot
2 tablespoons relish (Wickle recommended)
½ cup Thai sweet chile sauce
1½ tablespoons tarragon vinegar
¼ teaspoon chopped fresh tarragon
1 cup mayonnaise, preferably Lesieur
Salt and freshly ground black pepper to taste

Combine all ingredients and mix well.

SOUPS

Hot Asparagus Soup *62*

Black Bean Soup *64*

Crab Soup *66*

French Onion Soup *67*

Gazpacho *68*

Lobster Bisque *69*

Parsnip Minestrone *70*

Sweet Pea Soup *71*

Split Pea Soup *72*

Squash and Sweet Potato Soup *74*

Corn Soup *75*

Tortilla Soup *76*

White Bean Soup
with Escarole and Parmigiano *78*

Spanish Lentil Soup *79*

Cold Asparagus Soup *80*

Spiced Sweet Potato
and Ginger Soup *81*

HOT ASPARAGUS SOUP

WHAT MAKES THIS SOUP unique is the addition of fresh spinach, puréed with the cream and soft asparagus just before serving to add vibrant taste and color. Straining is also essential. The asparagus spears called for here can be either skinny or thick, although I do think it's important to use thick when asparagus is served on its own. For best results, weigh the asparagus after trimming the spears.

Makes 4 to 6 servings

18 diagonally cut 1-inch fresh asparagus tips
   (for garnish)
5 Tbsp. butter
5 Tbsp. flour
2 Tbsp. olive oil
1½ cups sliced yellow onions
2 Tbsp. chopped shallots
2 Tbsp. minced garlic
About 1 qt. (4 cups) chicken stock or broth
   (purchased or homemade)
1 Tbsp. salt
¼ tsp. white pepper
2 cups heavy cream
2½ lb. trimmed fresh asparagus, coarsely chopped
¾ lb. fresh spinach,
   washed with large stems removed

Cook asparagus tips in lightly salted boiling water in saucepan just until softened. Immediately place in bowl of ice water; let stand until cooled. Drain; reserve for garnish.

For roux, melt butter in small saucepan on medium heat. Add flour; cook 5 to 6 min. or until golden brown, whisking constantly. Remove from heat; set aside.

Heat oil in large saucepan on medium heat. Add yellow onions and shallots; sauté until softened. Add garlic; sauté a few minutes longer. Stir in chicken stock, salt and pepper; bring to boil. Add roux; cook until thickened, whisking constantly. Add cream and chopped asparagus; cook until tender. Remove from heat; cool slightly.

Add equal portions of soup and spinach to blender or food processor; blend until smooth. Add additional chicken stock if the soup seems too thick. Pour through strainer into serving bowl. Discard strained solids.

Serve soup garnished with reserved asparagus tips.

BLACK BEAN SOUP

JALAPEÑO PEPPER imparts a little heat to this variation on the classic, but what makes it unique is the addition of dry sherry, light soy sauce and liquid smoke. Creme fraiche and sliced scallions as garnishes contribute color and contrasting tastes. The recipe can be easily doubled if you're serving a crowd.

Makes 7½ cups or 5 to 6 servings

1 lb. dried black beans, soaked overnight
1½ qt. (6 cups) chicken stock or broth
*   (purchased or homemade)*
1 cup finely chopped onions
4 tsp. minced garlic
1 Tbsp. corn oil
1 cup finely chopped carrots
½ fresh jalapeño pepper, stem, membranes
*   and seeds removed, finely chopped*
1 bay leaf
2 tsp. salt
½ tsp. white pepper
¼ tsp. dried thyme leaves
⅓ cup dry sherry
2 Tbsp. lite soy sauce
½ tsp. liquid smoke
Crème fraîche (for garnish)
Scallions, sliced (for garnish)

Drain soaked beans; rinse with cold water. Place in stockpot. Add chicken stock; cook, partially covered, 1 to 1½ hours or until beans are tender, adding water if necessary to keep beans covered. Drain. Reserve 1 cup of the cooked beans for garnish. Return remaining beans to stockpot.

Sauté onions and garlic in hot oil in skillet just until tender. Add to beans in stockpot along with 2 cups water and all remaining ingredients except reserved beans and garnishes. Bring to boil; simmer, partially covered, 20 min. or until carrots are tender, occasionally skimming foam off surface.

Remove and discard bay leaf. Working in batches, purée soup in blender. Return to stockpot.

Ladle soup into serving bowls. Garnish with crème fraîche, scallions and reserved beans.

CRAB SOUP

MINOR'S CRAB BASE is the magic ingredient in this rich bisque, from a chef in Jacksonville, Fla., Richard Grenamayer; it produces a very deep crab taste. Sherry also enhances the seafood flavor. And, of course, lump crab laced into the soup just before serving also amplifies the eating experience.

Makes 6 to 8 servings

Crab Base
1 qt. (4 cups) water
5 tsp. Minor's Crab Base
2 tsp. Old Bay Seasoning

Soup
2 qt. (8 cups) half-and-half
2 tsp. butter
½ cup finely chopped onions
½ cup finely chopped celery
2 tsp. ground white pepper
Dash cayenne pepper
½ cup flour
1 cup cream sherry
¾ lb. crabmeat

Crab Base
Bring ingredients to boil in saucepan. Remove from heat.

Soup
Bring half-and-half just to simmer in saucepan. Keep warm over very low heat. Melt butter in Dutch oven over medium heat. Add vegetables, seasonings and Crab Base; stir. Cook 8 to 10 min. or until vegetables are softened. Add flour; stir until well blended. Stir in sherry. Gradually stir in warmed half-and-half. Reduce heat to medium-low; simmer until thickened, stirring frequently to prevent soup from burning.

Gently flake crabmeat. Add to soup; stir. Cook and stir until heated through.

FRENCH ONION SOUP

JOSH MOULTON, who some years ago was the chef at the Monkey Bar in Midtown Manhattan, was nice enough to share this recipe. The secret to stellar onion soup is slow-cooking the onions until they caramelize, and here that tedious task is simplified by baking rather than sautéing — all you have to do is remember to stir the pan occasionally over a couple of hours in the oven. Both sherry and brandy are also used, to bring out even more sweetness from the Vidalia onions.

Makes 6 to 8 servings

2 Tbsp. canola oil
2 Tbsp. butter
4½ lb. Vidalia onions (about 6 large), sliced
1 tsp. salt
¾ cup medium sherry
½ cup brandy
2 fresh thyme sprigs
1 bay leaf
2 qt. (8 cups) beef stock or broth
  (purchased or homemade)
Sourdough bread slices
2 cups grated Gruyère cheese

Heat oven to 400°F.

Brush oil onto bottom of large (at least 7-qt.) heavy-bottomed ovenproof Dutch oven. Add butter; cook on medium-low heat until melted. Stir in onions and salt; cover. Place in oven; bake 1 hour. (Onions will be moist and slightly reduced in volume.) Remove pan from oven. Stir to scrape onions from bottom and side of pan. Return to oven; bake, partially covered, 1½ to 1¾ hours or until onions are very soft and golden brown, stirring onions and scraping bottom and side of pan after 1 hour.

Remove pan from oven; place on top of stove. Cook onions, adding water ¼ cup at a time, until water is cooked off, stirring constantly to prevent onions from burning. Add sherry, brandy, thyme and bay leaf; cook until liquid is reduced by about half. Add beef stock; cook 30 min., occasionally skimming off any foam that rises to the surface. Remove and discard thyme sprigs and bay leaf.

Cut bread and cheese to fit tops of 6 to 8 ovenproof serving bowls. Toast both sides of bread slices under broiler. Top with cheese; broil until melted.

Ladle soup into serving bowls; top with cheese toasts.

GAZPACHO

I MAKE THIS sensational cold soup only between the middle of July and the beginning of September because the fabulous taste of tomatoes in that limited season is what makes it so very special. This was given to me by Pierre Mondard, who helped me with recipe development when I had restaurants at Bergdorf Goodman in New York and who was for years a chef at Lenotre in Paris. Beyond garnishing the soup with small cubed peppers in four colors, I very often put some lump crabmeat or marinated duck confit at the base of each bowl as a little serendipity.

Makes 6 to 8 servings

2 lb. (900 g) ripe tomatoes
7 oz. (200 g) seedless cucumbers, peeled
3.5 oz. (100 g) green bell pepper,
  seeded1.7 oz. (50 g) red onion
1 small garlic clove, peeled
4 oz. (90 g) tomato paste
2 oz. (57 g) ketchup
1.7 oz. (40 g) white bread, crust removed
5 tsp. sherry vinegar
8 to 10 drops Tabasco sauce
5 fresh basil leaves
1½ tsp. Salt
¼ tsp. black pepper
½ cup (100 g) olive oil
½ cup each cubed green,
  orange, red and yellow peppers (for garnish)
Basil chiffonade (for garnish)

Combine all ingredients except oil and garnishes. Add, in batches, to blender; blend until smooth. Strain through fine-mesh strainer, if necessary. Pour into large bowl.

Add oil gradually, whisking constantly until blended. Refrigerate until chilled. Garnish with peppers and basil chiffonade just before serving.

LOBSTER BISQUE

I USED TO GO to the all trouble of getting enough lobster shells to make this soup; I used to cajole fishmongers to save me shells so I could get the lobster taste. Then I discovered Minor's Lobster Base, which streamlines the production and intensifies the flavor. Josh Moulton, when he was the chef at the Monkey Bar in Midtown, gave me the ideas of thickening the soup with white rice and flavoring it with tarragon, Tabasco and sherry.

Makes 4 to 6 servings

Lobster Base
1½ qt. (6 cups) water
2 Tbsp. Minor's Lobster Base
1 Tbsp. Old Bay Seasoning

Soup
¼ cup olive oil
2 large onions, roughly chopped
2 celery stalks, roughly chopped
2 carrots, roughly chopped
Meat from 1 to 2 ooked lobsters (1½ to 2 lb. each)
2 oz. tomato paste
2 cups dry sherry
1cup brandy
1cup tomato pureé
1½ qt. (6 cups) chicken stock or broth
  (purchased or homemade)
1 bay leaf
½ cup uncooked white rice
1 to 1½ cups heavy cream
5 sprigs fresh tarragon

1 tsp. lemon juice
1 tsp. Tabasco sauce
Dash sweet sherry
Salt and pepper, to taste

Lobster Base
Bring ingredients to boil in saucepan. Remove from heat.

Soup
Heat oil in large saucepan over medium heat. Add vegetables; sauté 5 to 7 min. or until vegetables start to soften. Stir in tomato paste; cook 5 min., stirring constantly. Add sherry and brandy; cook until reduced by three-quarters. Add tomato pureé; cook 3 to 4 min. Add Lobster Base, chicken stock and bay leaf; simmer 1 hour. Strain liquid; discard strained solids. Return strained liquid to saucepan.

Add rice to strained liquid; cook 20 min. or until tender. Add, in batches, to blender; blend until smooth. (Note: If rice isn't thoroughly blended, strain through coarse strainer; discard strained rice. Return strained soup to pan.) Stir in 1 cup cream; simmer 5 min. (If soup is too thick, add remaining ½ cup cream.)

Wrap tarragon in cheesecloth. Add to soup along with the lemon juice, Tabasco sauce and sherry; stir. Simmer 10 min. Season with salt and pepper. Remove cheesecloth with tarragon; discard.

Place 4 or 5 bite-size pieces of lobster in each shallow dish; cover with soup.

PARSNIP MINESTRONE

LEO PULITO, the proprietor of Petrarca Cucina, at White and Church Streets in TriBeCa for years owned Arqua, across the street. When I first started going there with Ed Mills — to my mind one of America's best architects, who happened to do my house in Bridgehampton — Leo gave me this recipe. There are lots of minestrones, but the special ingredient in Leo's is the parsnips. So many cooks, even those who are experienced, don't appreciate the sweetness those roots contribute. Smaller ones are best because you do not have to cut out the cores.

Makes 6 to 8 servings

1½ cups chopped carrots, medium dice
1½ cups chopped celery, medium dice
1½ cups chopped yellow onions, small dice
¼ cup olive oil, divided use
5 cups peeled, chopped Yukon Gold potatoes,
*   medium dice*
5 cups peeled, chopped parsnips, medium dice
5 plum tomatoes,
*   fresh or canned, quartered, seeded*
¼ cup tomato paste
10 to 12 cups chicken stock or broth
*   (purchased or homemade) or water, divided use*
3 to 4 cups thickly chopped escarole
*   (green parts only)*
3 garlic cloves, minced
Salt and pepper, to taste
Freshly grated Parmigiano Reggiano for garnish

Sauté carrots, celery and onions in 3 Tbsp. hot oil in large saucepan 3 to 5 min. Add potatoes; sauté 3 to 5 min. Add parsnips; sauté 2 min.

Stir in tomatoes and tomato paste; cook 3 min., stirring constantly. Add enough chicken stock to cover vegetables buy about 3 inches; simmer until reduced by half. Add remaining stock, 1 cup at a time, cooking until vegetables are softened and broth is cooked to desired consistency, skimming foam from surface as needed. (Add more stock if you prefer a less thick soup.) Meanwhile, heat remaining oil in large skillet. Add escarole and garlic; sauté until softened. Stir into soup. Season with salt and pepper. Garnish with Parmigiano.

SWEET PEA SOUP

MY FRIEND BERNARD SICHEL, who was building the Cigna health building in Glendale, California, with me, introduced me to Far Niente, the restaurant there that shared this recipe. Sweet potatoes give it an unusual flavor. As always, if you want a thinner soup add more stock.

Makes 8 to 10 servings

3 cups chopped onions, medium chop
1½ cups chopped celery, medium chop
1 cup chopped carrots, small chop
3 Tbsp. butter
About 3 qt. (12 cups) chicken stock or broth
  (purchased or homemade)
2 cups (6 oz.) chopped peeled sweet potatoes,
  medium chop
2½ Tbsp. chopped fresh parsley
2½ Tbsp. lite soy sauce
2 tsp. salt
½ Tbsp. onion powder
⅛ tsp. white pepper
2¾ lb. frozen petite peas
4 sprigs fresh parsley

Sauté onions, celery and carrots in melted butter in 5-qt. Dutch oven over medium heat until the onions are translucent but the vegetables are not browned.

Add all remaining ingredients except peas and parsley; stir. Simmer until potatoes are tender.

Add peas and parsley; simmer until peas are heated through. Skim off any foam that rises to the surface. Purée soup, in batches if necessary, in food processor or blender. If the soup is too thick, think with additional warmed stock. Adjust seasoning, if necessary.

SPLIT PEA SOUP

PARSNIPS AND LEEKS give a sophisticated flavor to this soup, which also gets richness from the hambone simmered with the peas. (You can leave it out, but the soup really is best with it in.) Rosemary-seasoned croutons made from brioche also help.

Makes 6 servings

Garnish
4 slices thick-cut bacon

Croutons
4 slices brioche or white bread, crusts trimmed
6 Tbsp. butter
1 tsp. chopped fresh rosemary
¼ tsp. freshly ground black pepper
½ tsp. salt

Bouquet Garni
6 sprigs fresh parsley
3 sprigs fresh thyme
5 whole black peppercorns
1 bay leaf

Soup
About 4 Tbsp. olive oil
1 large carrot, small dice
½ medium yellow onion, small dice
2 stalks celery, small dice
1 medium leek, small dice
  (white and light green parts only)
1 small parsnip, small dice
1 clove garlic, minced
1 lb. dried split peas, blanched
1 hambone
1 tsp. salt
2½ qt. (10 cups) chicken stock or broth
  (purchased or homemade), adding more if needed

Garnish
Heat the oven to 375 degrees. Lay bacon slices on a sheet of parchment on a baking sheet and bake until crisp, turning once. Drain off and reserve any fat.

Croutons
Cut bread into ¼-inch cubes. Melt butter in large sauté pan over medium heat. When foam subsides, add bread; cook until golden brown, stirring occasionally. Cool slightly. Place bread in large resealable plastic bag. Add rosemary, pepper and salt. Close bag; shake gently to evenly coat bread cubes with herb mixture.

Bouquet Garni
Wrap ingredients in cheesecloth; tie closed with kitchen string.

Soup

Add reserved bacon fat to Dutch oven or stockpot. Add enough olive oil to make ¼ cup. Heat over medium heat. Add carrots, onions, celery, leeks, parsnips and garlic; sauté 5 to 7 min. or until vegetables are softened but not browned. Add split peas, hambone, salt and Bouquet Garni; stir. Cook 5 min. Stir in chicken stock; bring to boil. Simmer, partially covered, on low heat 1 hour or until peas are softened, skimming foam from surface of soup as needed and adding more chicken stock if soup becomes too thick.

Remove bouquet garni and ham bone. Remove any meat remaining on ham bone; trim off any sinew. Chop the meat and reserve for garnish. Discard bone and bouquet garni. Blend soup, in small batches, in blender until smooth. Adjust seasoning, if necessary. Coarsely chop bacon. Garnish filled bowls of soup with chopped ham, bacon and Croutons.

TIP
• *If soup is too thick, add more chicken stock or water until it reaches desired consistency.*

SQUASH AND SWEET POTATO SOUP

ACORN SQUASH roasted with a sugar cure forms the base of this fall harvest soup, which is also enhanced by butternut squash plus sweet potatoes and apples. Leeks, sage, ginger and especially Calvados intensify the flavors.

Makes about 12 servings

2 Tbsp. plus 2 tsp. light brown sugar
2 Tbsp. butter, softened
$1/8$ tsp. salt
1 acorn squash, cut in half, seeds removed
3 sprigs fresh sage, chopped
¼ tsp. minced garlic
¼ cup peanut oil
1 medium leek, well washed,
    white and light green parts roughly chopped
1 yellow onion, peeled, roughly chopped
    (about 1½ cups)
2 celery stalks, roughly chopped
1 tsp. grated ginger
1 small sweet potato, peeled, roughly chopped
    (about 1½ cups)
1 small butternut squash, peeled, cut in half,
    seeds and area around seeds removed,
    then remaining squash roughly chopped
    (about 4 cups)
2 qt. (8 cups) chicken stock or broth
    (purchased or homemade)
½ cup Calvados
1½ Tbsp. salt
1 Tbsp. butter
1 Tbsp. olive oil
1 Granny Smith apple, peeled,
    cored and cut into ½-inch cubes

1 cup heavy cream
¼ tsp. white pepper
Chopped fresh chives (for garnish)

Heat oven to 400°F.

Mix brown sugar, butter and salt until mixture forms a paste; spoon evenly into both acorn squash shells. Place, cut sides up, in baking dish filled with ½ inch of water. Bake 30 min. or until squash is tender. Cool. Pour brown sugar paste from shells into bowl. Scrape pulp from shells into same bowl; mix well. Discard shells.

Sauté sage and garlic in hot peanut oil in large saucepan 2 min. Add leeks, onions, celery and ginger; sauté 2 min. Add sweet potato, butternut squash and acorn squash mixture; sauté 2 min.

Add chicken stock, Calvados and salt; stir. Bring to a boil. Reduce heat and simmer 40 min., skimming foam from surface as needed. Remove from heat; cool 15 to 20 min.

Add cream and white pepper to soup. Add to blender in batches; blend until smooth. Check and adjust seasoning if necessary.

Meanwhile, melt butter with olive oil in small sauté pan over high heat. Add apples; sauté 3 to 5 min. or until lightly browned.

Ladle soup into shallow bowls; top with apples. Garnish with chives.

CORN SOUP

BECAUSE GOOD CORN is so essential here, I make this soup only between July and early September, when the Long Island crop is at its peak. A smidgeon of sugar and a squeeze of lime juice bring out the sweetness, as does the coconut milk.

Makes 4 to 5 servings

6 Tbsp. butter
2 medium onions, medium dice
½ cup chopped carrots, medium dice
½ cup chopped celery, medium dice
2 garlic cloves, finely chopped
8 cups fresh corn kernels (from about 8 ears)
2 tsp. garam masala
1 tsp. ground turmeric
1 qt. (4 cups) chicken stock
   (purchased or homemade)
2 cups coconut milk
2 tsp. sugar
4 tsp. lime juice
Salt and white pepper, to taste
Chopped chives or scallion greens, for garnish
1 cup blanched corn kernels, for garnish

Melt butter in large saucepan over medium heat. Add next 4 ingredients; sauté 5 min. or until tender. Add corn, garam masala and turmeric; stir. Cook 3 min., stirring frequently.

Add chicken stock, coconut milk and sugar. Bring to boil; simmer 15 min. Remove from heat.

Pour, in small batches, into blender; blend until smooth. Strain, then return to saucepan. Stir in lime juice, salt and pepper. Garnish each portion with either chives or scallion greens and a few corn kernels.

TORTILLA SOUP

OVER MY LIFETIME I have spent many years living in the Beverly Hills Hotel in Los Angeles. At one point eight or 10 years ago, Pepe de Anda, the director of the Polo Lounge, shared this recipe. When I went back two or three years ago, I commented that it did not taste as fabulous as it once did. He agreed — the old chef had taken the recipe. So I returned what he had given me, and they are now back to cooking it the right way. Part of what makes this soup so impressive is the garnishing: the chicken breast, avocado and shredded Cheddar, plus flour tortillas (not the usual corn ones) lightly fried and paired with scallions.

Makes 4 to 6 servings

Soup
3 Tbsp. olive oil
*10½ oz. (300 g) onions
    (about 2 medium), chopped*
3½ oz. (100 g) celery (about 4 stalks), chopped
3½ oz. (100 g) carrots, chopped
*3½ oz. (100 g) leeks,
    white and green parts chopped*
1 shallot, chopped
2 garlic cloves, mashed
*10½ oz. (300 g) red peppers (about 5),
    seeded, cored and medium chopped*
*3½ oz. (100 g) poblano sweet peppers,
    soaked in water for 15 min., then seeded,
    cored and medium chopped*
*1½ oz. (40 g) fresh jalapeño pepper,
    seeded, medium chopped*
*1¼ cups (300 mL) drained canned
    plum tomatoes*
3 Tbsp. tomato paste
*6 small white corn tortillas (6 inch),
    roughly chopped*
½ cup chopped fresh cilantro
1 tsp. dried oregano leaves
1 tsp. dried thyme leaves
1 tsp. ground cumin
*2 qt. (8 cups) chicken stock or broth
    (purchased or homemade)*
Salt and black pepper, to taste

Garnishes

2 tsp. freshly ground black pepper
1 cup chopped cooked chicken breast
1 cup chopped avocados
1 cup shredded cheddar cheese
5 flour tortillas (8 inch), cut into thin strips,
  lightly fried in vegetable oil
½ cup sliced scallions (green parts only)

Soup

Heat oil in large stockpot. Add onions, celery, carrots and leeks; sauté 5 to 10 min. or until partially softened. Add shallots and garlic; sauté for a few minutes longer.

Add all remaining soup ingredients except salt and black pepper; stir. Simmer 30 min. or until fresh vegetables are softened, occasionally skimming off any foam that rises to the surface.

Purée soup, in batches if necessary, in blender or food processor. Strain soup. Season with salt and black pepper. If the soup is too thick, gradually stir in additional chicken stock until soup is of desired consistency.

Serve with garnishes as desired.

WHITE BEAN SOUP

THIS LOOKS VERY straightforward until you notice what makes the broth special: A chunk of Parmigiano-Reggiano rind that simmers with the beans to give that great umami flavor without chicken or beef bones. Escarole sautéed with garlic adds color and extra flavor.

Makes 6 to 8 servings

2 cups dried cannellini beans, soaked overnight
2 qt. (8 cups) chicken stock or broth
   (purchased or homemade)
1 qt. (4 cups) water
1 piece Parmesan cheese rind (5x2 inch)
1 bay leaf
4 cups escarole
3 garlic cloves, finely chopped
Salt and pepper, to taste

Place beans in Dutch oven. Add chicken stock, water, Parmesan rind and bay leaf; stir. Bring to boil over high heat. Reduce heat; simmer vigorously 1 to 1¼ hours or until beans are completely softened and liquid begins to thicken, stirring occasionally. Skim off any foam that rises to surface. Remove and discard Parmesan rind and bay leaf.

Purée the soup, in batches if necessary, in food processor or blender. Add more water or chicken stock if soup is too thick.

Sauté escarole and garlic in sauté pan until escarole starts to wilt. Add to soup; stir. Adjust seasoning with salt and pepper, if necessary.

TIP
• *To soak the beans, dissolve 3 Tbsp. salt in 1 gal. cold water in large bowl. Add beans; let stand at room temperature at least 8 hours, or up to 24 hours. Drain and rinse well.*

SPANISH LENTIL SOUP

I GO TO PANAMA often to develop housing, and I always stay at the Bristol Hotel, where Cuquita (Coketa) Arias was the chef for many years. This wholesome soup is her recipe. Chorizo makes it come alive. Because this is so filling, serve it either as a main course or in dainty portions as a starter.

Makes 6 to 8 servings

1 lb. (454 g) green lentils, preferably French
¼ cup olive oil
1 medium onion, finely chopped
3 garlic cloves
1 Tbsp. chopped fresh thyme
1 Tbsp. salt
2 tsp. ground black pepper
1 tsp. ground cumin
1 lb. (454 g) carrots, ¼-inch dice
8 celery stalks, finely chopped
2 qt. (8 cups) chicken stock or broth
   (purchased or homemade), or more if necessary
¼ cup tomato paste
¾ lb. (340 g) to 1 lb. (454 g) Spanish chorizo,
   ¼-inch dice
2 Tbsp. white vinegar
Freshly grated Parmigiano-Reggiano

Place lentils in large bowl. Add enough boiling water to completely cover lentils. Let stand 15 min.; drain.

Heat oil in large saucepan over medium heat. Add onions, garlic, thyme, salt, pepper and cumin; mix well. Cook 20 min. or until onions are translucent, stirring frequently. Add carrots and celery; cook 5 min., stirring frequently.

Add 2 qt. chicken stock, tomato paste and lentils; stir. Cover. Bring to boil. Simmer, uncovered, over medium-low heat 1 hour, stirring occasionally and adding additional stock if necessary for thinner consistency.

Add chorizo and vinegar; stir. Simmer 5 min. Serve topped with Parmesan cheese. Drizzle with a little additional olive oil if desired.

COLD ASPARAGUS SOUP

IMPROBABLE AS IT SEEMS, the dry ranch dressing mix here is what gives a special flavor to this soup, which I discovered at the Washington Duke Inn in North Carolina. Other surprising ingredients include agave syrup, Champagne vinegar and buttermilk.

Makes about 10 servings

2 bunches fresh asparagus spears (about 2 lb.),
   roughly chopped
2 cups vegetable or chicken stock
   (purchased or homemade)
½ cup agave syrup or honey
¼ cup champagne vinegar
2 cups buttermilk
1 cup heavy cream
2 tsp. dry ranch dressing and dip mix
½ tsp. ground coriander
¼ tsp. ground allspice
Pinch cayenne pepper
Salt and pepper (to taste)

Cook asparagus in lightly salted boiling water in saucepan just until softened. Immediately place in bowl of ice water; let stand until cooled.

Use blender to blend asparagus, vegetable stock, agave syrup and vinegar until smooth; pour through strainer into large bowl.

Add remaining ingredients; whisk until blended.

SPICED SWEET POTATO AND GINGER SOUP

A NORTH CAROLINA chef from Greensboro, Oliver Lloyd, was kind enough to share this.

Makes 8 servings

4 medium sweet potatoes,
  peeled and cut into 1-inch cubes
2 tablespoons olive oil
2 tablespoons salted butter
1 cup onions, chopped
3 cloves garlic, minced
½ teaspoon nutmeg
½ teaspoon cardamom
1 tablespoon honey
2 teaspoons ground ginger
2 teaspoons salt
5 cups chicken stock
1½ cups heavy cream (or whole milk)
Greek yogurt or sour cream for garnish (optional)

Preheat oven to 400°. Place sweet potatoes on a baking sheet lined with parchment paper. Drizzle with 1 tablespoon of olive oil and sprinkle with salt. Cook 30 minutes, or until edges are lightly browned.

In a stockpot, heat butter and remaining olive oil. Stir in onions. Cook onions for 5 to 10 minutes. Add garlic, nutmeg, cardamom, honey, and ginger. Stir and cook for 2 minutes. Stir in sweet potatoes, remaining salt, and chicken stock. Simmer 20 minutes.

Working in small batches, process mixture in a blender until smooth. Add soup back to pot and stir in heavy cream. Simmer on low heat for 5 minutes. Serve hot and garnish with Greek yogurt or sour cream.

PASTA

Lasagne With Meat Sauce *84*
Pasta Dough for Filled Pasta *86*
Quadrettine *88*
Risotto Milanese *89*
Linguine With Morel Sauce *90*

LASAGNE WITH MEAT SAUCE

MIXING THE MEAT sauce with the béchamel makes a huge difference with my lasagne. The big thing is getting the pasta and filling to work in the pan. A 9- by 6-inch dish is optimal; if yours is a little smaller or a little bigger you can use less or more of the meat-and-béchamel mixture and cut the pasta sheets to fit. If you find yourself with extra sauce, just add another layer of pasta. Store-bought pasta can be used if you don't have time to make the dough; just find the thinnest possible, fresh or dry.

Makes 6 to 8 servings

Meat Sauce
¼ cup extra-virgin olive oil
⅓ cup minced Spanish onion
⅓ cup minced parsnip
⅓ cup minced carrot
⅓ cup minced celery
1 clove garlic, minced
6 oz. ground beef
6 oz. lean ground pork
8 oz. Italian sausage (without fennel seeds),
  casings removed, crumbled
2 oz. thinly sliced pancetta, minced
2 oz. thinly sliced prosciutto, minced
2 cups chicken stock (purchased or homemade)
1½ cups dry white wine
2 cups Pummarola/Tomato Sauce
Salt and freshly ground black pepper,
  to taste

Béchamel
3 Tbsp. butter
¼ cup minced onions
3 Tbsp. flour
1½ cups milk
Pinch salt
⅛ tsp. white pepper

Pasta Dough for Filled Pasta (page 86)

Lasagne Assembly
½ cup grated Parmigiano-Reggiano
3 Tbsp. butter, cubed

Meat Sauce
Heat oil in large saucepan over medium heat. Add vegetables; cook 5 to 6 min. or until lightly browned, stirring frequently. Add meats; cook 7 to 8 min. or until done, stirring frequently. Stir in chicken stock and wine; cook until most of the liquid is cooked off. Add Pummarola/Tomato Sauce; stir. Season with salt and pepper. Bring to boil. Reduce heat to low; simmer, partially covered, 1½ to 2 hours or until thickened, stirring every 10 min. Add a little water if it starts to thicken too much.

Béchamel

Melt butter in medium saucepan over low heat. Add onions; sauté 5 min. or until tender. (Be careful not to burn.) Add flour; whisk until blended. Cook over medium heat 5 min. or until mixture turns a light, golden sandy color. Meanwhile, heat milk in separate saucepan. Add hot milk, 1 cup at a time, to flour mixture, whisking constantly until sauce is well blended. Bring sauce to simmer; cook 10 min., stirring constantly. Remove from heat. Season with salt and white pepper.

Pasta Dough

Prepare dough as directed for lasagna.

Lasagne Assembly

Heat oven to 400°F. Mix Meat Sauce and Béchamel Sauce until blended. Butter bottom and sides of 9- by 6-inch glass dish. Place pasta sheet on bottom of prepared dish; cover with thin layer of sauce. Sprinkle lightly with Parmigiano-Reggiano. Repeat layers until you have at least 5 layers. Top final layer with several dollops of butter. Bake 15 min. or until heated through.

PASTA DOUGH FOR FILLED PASTA

THIS TECHNIQUE was given to me by Giuliano Bugialli, who taught me when he was helping me prepare the menu for the restaurant on the seventh floor of Bergdorf Goodman that subsequently never came to be. He had reassuring advice on what type of flour to use: Very often, unbleached white flour as he calls for here is just as good as the esoteric flours, like 00, that some recipes insist on.

Makes enough for one pan of Lasagne if the dough is rolled out at the thinnest setting

1 cup unbleached flour
1 extra-large egg
1 tsp. oil
Pinch of saffron
Pinch of salt

Pasta Dough
Mound flour on work surface; let stand 15 min. to remove excess air.

Make well in center of flour. Break egg into small bowl. Whisk in oil, saffron and salt until blended. Pour into well in flour. Starting at outside edge of well, use spoon to start mixing in flour from around edge of well just until pasta is no longer wet. (Note: Continue to work from side of well, pressing down as lightly as possible with spoon to blend in the egg mixture. Only about $^2/_3$ cup of the flour will be used to make the dough. Dough should hold together and not be sticky.)

After dough is dry enough to easily work with, gather the remaining flour and put it through a strainer. Hold strainer close to the board when straining it so that you don't aerate the flour. *(Do not sift—you are removing lumps, not aerating it.)* Use this strained flour when preparing the pasta dough in the pasta machine. (See steps 2 and 7 below.)

Pasta Machine
(used to knead the prepared Pasta Dough)

1. *Set pasta machine at widest setting*
2. *Lightly flour one side of pasta.*
3. *Make tri-fold (puff pastry fold) with floured-side on the outside. (If preparing a large quantity, use 2 folds.)*
4. *Press air out with fingers going in one direction.*
5. *Flour, fold, press and roll 4 more times using the highest setting.*
6. *After 5 runs at the thickest setting, then start going down one setting at a time.*
7. *Lightly flour both sides of dough. Do not fold. Put dough through the rollers once at each setting, lightly flouring each time.*

For Cannelloni/Lasagne
Let Pasta Dough rest on clean cotton towel until film forms on top. Cut pasta into desired shape. Cover with additional towel. Add to salted boiling water; cook 30 sec. or until al dente.

Immediately submerge dough in bowl of ice water; let stand 1 min. Remove from water; drain. Fold in towel. Refrigerate until ready to use.

For Ravioli
Let Pasta Dough rest on clean cotton towel until film forms on top.

Spoon stuffing between pasta sheets, then use cutter to cut into squares. (Cut squares will stick together – no egg or water is needed to seal them.)

Store ravioli in single layer on parchment paper or in lightly floured sheet pan. Refrigerate or freeze until ready to cook.

Add to pan of salted boiling water; cook 1 to 2 min. or until al dente.

TIPS
• *The saffron is used to add color to the pasta dough.*

• *In addition to adding both texture and flavor to the pasta dough, the salt also helps prevent the dough from crumbling.*

• *The pasta dough is the softest when prepared with oil, then milk, then water.*

• *Pasta is first a thin batter, then a thick batter and then a dough.*

• *Humidity will affect the pasta dough. It will take longer to prepare the pasta dough if preparing in a humid climate.*

QUADRETTINE

THIS SIMPLE RECIPE using crisped prosciutto and baby spinach was given to me by a restaurant that used to be on 53rd Street between Second and Third Avenues, called San Marino. It closed at least 25 years ago, but this was their best dish, and they were nice enough to share the recipe with me. This makes just enough for two, but the recipe can be doubled.

Makes 2 dinner-size servings

*8 to 10 oz. fresh baby spinach,
    cleaned, thick stems removed*
*6 oz. prosciutto (¹/₈ inch thick),
    excess fat trimmed*
2 Tbsp. olive oil
*½ cup chicken stock or broth
    (purchased or homemade)*
9 oz. fresh fettuccine
¼ cup butter, room temperature
½ cup grated Parmigiano-Reggiano
Salt and pepper, to taste

Sauté ¹/₃ of the spinach in large skillet on low heat just until spinach starts to wilt. Gradually add remaining spinach, cooking after each batch just until spinach starts to wilt. Immediately add to ice water bath to cool. Drain, then squeeze dry. Cut into medium chop.

Cut prosciutto into 4-inch pieces. Heat oil in large sauté pan. Add prosciutto; sauté until crisp and well browned. (Be careful not to burn.) Add chicken stock; cook until reduced by half.

Meanwhile, cook pasta in boiling salted water.

Drain pasta. Add to prosciutto mixture along with the spinach and butter; mix well. Stir in Parmigiano-Reggiano. Season with salt and pepper.

TIP
• Prepare using baby spinach so you don't need to clean it and trim the stems.

RISOTTO MILANESE

I WAS CRAZY about the risotto in a small restaurant in Milan many years ago and they gave me this recipe. It's not so different from a lot of other recipes, but it's so good I hesitate to try to improve on it. The whole trick is to use very hot stock and add it gradually so that the grains of rice don't drown; add more only when the previous batch has been absorbed. If you're making this for company, you can do what chefs do: Cook the rice until it's almost softened, hold it for several hours in the refrigerator, then reheat while adding the remaining cup or so of stock just before serving. Always heat the plates before serving.

Makes 4 to 6 servings

4 to 5 cups hot chicken stock
  (purchased or homemade), divided use
1 to 2 tsp. small saffron grains,
  or more if you prefer
2 Tbsp. olive oil
¼ cup butter, divided use
½ small onion, chopped
1¼ cups Arborio or Carnaroli rice
1 cup dry white wine
5 to 6 Tbsp. grated Parmigiano-Reggiano

Remove about 1 Tbsp. hot stock and place in small bowl. Crumble in saffron and mix well. Set aside for later use. Keep remaining stock hot until ready to use.

Heat oil with 2 Tbsp. butter in medium saucepan over medium heat. Add onions; sauté 3 min.

Add rice; mix well. Cook 1 min. or until heated through, stirring constantly. Add wine; cook and stir 2 min. Add remaining chicken stock, 1 cup at a time, cooking after each addition until almost all the stock is absorbed and rice is tender.

Stir in saffron, Parmigiano-Reggiano and remaining 2 Tbsp. butter. Serve immediately.

LINGUINE WITH MOREL SAUCE

I DEVELOPED this sauce through much (pleasurable) experimentation to get the proportions right. The amount of morels is just a suggestion; use as many as you can afford (I have used up to 4 ounces). You could also serve this over porcini ravioli. I sometimes mix in shredded, cooked chicken, or just substitute chicken for the pasta.

Makes 2 to 3 servings

1¼ cups dried morels
½ cup white wine
1 clove garlic, minced
2 tablespoons finely chopped shallots
½ cup chicken stock
1½ cups heavy cream
Salt and freshly ground black pepper to taste
½ pound fresh linguine, cooked al dente

Rinse morels to remove grit. Cut into bite-size pieces.

Combine wine, shallots and garlic in saucepan and cook until reduced by half; be careful not to let burn. Add stock and continue cooking until reduced by half. Add morels and cream to pan; cook until morels are softened and sauce is thickened.

The Dining Room
Graphite and ink on Japan paper • Paul Signac, Paris 1886–87
Robert Lehman Collection, 1975

The Fish–monger
Polychrome woodblock print • Torii Kiyonaga, Japanese, Edo period (1615–1868)
H. O. Havemeyer Collection, 1929

SEAFOOD

Bay Scallops With Mussels Sauce *94*

Fillet of Sole With Pine Nut Crust *96*

Seared Tuna al Piment *98*

Seared Tuna Cylinder
With Beijing Sauce *100*

Slow-Cooked Salmon
With Brussels Sprouts *102*

Deviled Crab *103*

Tuna With Avocado Risotto
and Kaffir Sauce *104*

Fairview Jumbo Lump Crab Cakes
With Pickled Okra Aioli *106*

Sea Scallops Wrapped in Bacon
With Mussels Sauce *109*

Panko-Crusted Salmon With Cashews
and Honey Mustard *110*

BAY SCALLOPS WITH MUSSELS SAUCE

I ONLY MAKE SCALLOPS between November and early March as I find Nantucket Bay scallops are so much better that they are worth waiting for. The sauce is extremely good — mussels can be very salty, so you have to be willing to use a lot of cream; otherwise the flavor may be too intense. The leftover mussels make wonderful hors d'oeuvres when served on toothpicks with Mustard Sauce (page 47).

Makes 4 to 6 servings

Mussels Sauce
2 Tbsp. butter
2 shallots, finely chopped
1 cup dry white wine
5 lb. mussels, beards removed
1 cup heavy cream
Salt and black pepper, to taste (optional)

Scallops
80 to 90 bay scallops (Nantucket preferred)
1½ cups flour
4 tsp. kosher salt
2 tsp. black pepper
3 Tbsp. butter
2 Tbsp. peanut oil
½ cup-finely chopped fresh chives (for garnish)

Mussels Sauce
Melt butter in large saucepan. Add shallots; sauté 3 min. or until translucent. Stir in wine; simmer 2 min. Add mussels; cook until opened, stirring frequently. Remove and discard any unopened mussels. Remove remaining mussels from pan, reserving liquid in pan. Remove mussels from shells; discard shells. Refrigerate mussels for another us, such as hors d'oeuvres or seafood salad. Strain the juice and cook until reduced by half, or until sauce reaches desired thickness. (The sauce can be made ahead to this point and refrigerated.) Remove from heat and add cream; simmer until thickened, stirring constantly. Season with salt and pepper, if desired. Keep warm.

Scallops
Season scallops with salt and pepper. Toss scallops, in batches, with flour until evenly coated, then place in strainer; shake gently to remove excess flour.

Cook butter and oil in large sauté pan until butter is melted and foam subsides. Add scallops; sauté 2 to 3 min. or until evenly browned on both sides (Be careful not to burn scallops.).

Assembly
Pour Mussels Sauce into 4 rimmed plates. Add Scallops. Garnish with chives.

FILLET OF SOLE WITH PINE NUT CRUST

THIS RECIPE was given to me by Gloria Ciccarone-Nehls, who used to be the chef at the Huntington Hotel in San Francisco. I'm usually only enthusiastic about shellfish, but this gives enough flavor to the fillet of sole to make it worth the effort. Spinach, corn, sun-dried tomatoes and basil chiffonade complete the plate.

Makes 4 servings

Sauce
¹/₃ cup finely chopped shallots
1 cup dry white wine
1 lb. butter, cut into 10 to 12 pieces
¾ cup heavy cream
Zest and 3 Tbsp. juice from 1 lemon
Salt and pepper, to taste
1 to 2 Tbsp. cornstarch (optional)

Fish
¾ cup garlic-flavored croutons
¼ cup pine nuts, toasted
4 gray sole fillets (7 oz. each)
Salt and pepper, to taste
2 Tbsp. each butter and olive oil
  (add more, if necessary)
2 tsp. Dijon mustard
1¼ lb. (567 g) fresh baby spinach
3 cups blanched fresh corn kernels
½ cup sun-dried tomatoes, medium dice
½ cup fresh basil chiffonade

Sauce
Cook shallots in wine in medium saucepan on medium heat until wine is reduced by half. Gradually add butter, whisking after each addition until melted and well blended. Remove from heat.

Slowly whisk in cream until well blended. Return to heat; simmer 10 min. Add lemon zest, juice, salt and pepper. If sauce is not thick enough, mix cornstarch and enough water (1 to 2 Tbsp.) to make slurry. Gradually whisk into sauce and cook until thickened, stirring constantly. (Note: Sauce should be hot but not boiling when adding the slurry.)

Fish
Heat oven to 400°F.

Place croutons and pine nuts in food processor; pulse 10 to 20 sec. or just until roughly chopped.

Season fish with salt and pepper. Fold each fillet into thirds.

Melt butter with oil in medium nonstick sauté pan on medium-high heat. Add fish; cook 1 min. on each side or until seared on both sides. Transfer to shallow pan.

Bake 4 min. Spread fish with mustard; top with crumb mixture. Bake additional 3 to 4 min. or until fish flakes easily with fork.

To Plate

Spoon ¼ of the spinach onto center of each of 4 dinner plates; spread ¼ each of the corn and tomatoes around spinach. Top with Fish. Drizzle with Sauce; garnish with basil.

TIP

• *To toast the pine nuts, spread nuts onto bottom of shallow pan. Bake in 300°F oven 8 min. or until lightly toasted, shaking pan occasionally to prevent nuts from burning.*

SEARED TUNA AL PIMENT

THE RECIPE FOR THIS DISH, which has great taste and looks very attractive, was given to me by Jean Claude Dufour, the chef at Restaurant L'Esprit in St. Barts. I taste as I apply the piment d'Espelette to the tuna to be sure it's not too spicy. The tuna should be well-done outside, nearly raw inside. I slice it into one-inch slabs, sear them on each side, and then slice the tuna into strips — visually this resembles a strip of seared, very rare steak. Serve it with Asian Spring Roll Sauce (page 42).

Makes 4 servings

2 lb. tuna, sinew removed and discarded
1½ Tbsp. A.O.P piment d'Espelette
1½ tsp. kosher salt
1½ tsp. coarse ground white pepper
6 Tbsp. or more olive oil
Asian Spring Roll Sauce

Cut tuna into 4 rectangles, being careful not to lose too much tuna. Freeze 20 min.

Heat large skillet over medium-high heat until very hot. Meanwhile, mix piment d'espelette, salt and pepper. Sprinkle over both sides of tuna pieces, then press gently into tuna to secure.

Dip both sides of each tuna piece in olive oil. Add to hot skillet. Cook 1 min. on each side or just until long enough to sear tuna to deep color. (Do not overcook – tuna should be very rare.)

Remove tuna from skillet; cut diagonally into ½-inch-thick slices. Arrange on plates in crisscross pattern. Serve with Asian Spring Roll Sauce on the side.

TIP
• *Freezing the tuna before cooking it allows you to sear the tuna without overcooking it. For best results, use tongs when turning the tuna in the skillet.*

SEARED TUNA CYLINDER WITH BEIJING SAUCE

THIS RECIPE was given to me by Cuquita (Coketa) Arias, the chef at the Bristol Hotel in Panama who recently left to be chef at the new restaurant in the Canal Zone. The tuna is marinated and rolled and then placed in the freezer for 10 to 15 minutes so that it sears without overcooking. It's a very good dish.

Makes 4 servings

Tuna & Marinade
¼ cup soy sauce
4 tsp. lemon juice
4 tsp. sesame oil
4 tsp. finely chopped ginger
4 blocks of tuna (about 4 x ½ x ½ inch),
sinew section removed and reserved for another use

Beijing Sauce
1½ cups hoisin sauce
¼ cup honey
¼ cup soy sauce
¼ cup rice vinegar
¼ cup vegetable oil
4 scallions, tough green parts removed
and remaining scallion parts finely chopped
3 cloves garlic, finely chopped
1 tsp. finely chopped ginger

Tuna Preparation
About ½ cup each white and black sesame seeds
2 to 4 Tbsp. olive oil
(amount needed depends on size of pan used)

Marinade
Mix soy sauce, lemon juice, sesame oil and ginger in shallow dish. Add tuna; turn to evenly coat both sides of each block. Refrigerate 30 min. to marinate. Meanwhile, prepare Beijing Sauce.

Beijing Sauce
Bring all ingredients to boil in saucepan. Remove from heat; cool.

Tuna Preparation

Remove tuna from marinade; discard marinade. Coat tuna evenly with combined sesame seeds. Place each block of tuna on 12-inch-long sheet of plastic wrap; roll up tightly to form cylindrical shape. Freeze 10 to 15 min., then, if you have time, refrigerate for 30 minutes more.

Heat large skillet until very hot. Add oil; tilt skillet to evenly coat bottom with oil. Add tuna; cook 1 to 2 min. or until evenly seared. (Do not overcook. The meat inside each piece of tuna should be very rare.)

Pat tuna dry with paper towels. Cut diagonally in half; layer onto serving plates. Serve topped with Beijing Sauce.

TIPS

• *Beijing Sauce can be prepared ahead of time. Refrigerate up to 1 week before using.*

• *Chilling the tuna will allow it to be seared without overcooking it.*

• *Serve with your choice of hot cooked green vegetables.*

SLOW-COOKED SALMON WITH BRUSSELS SPROUTS

THE TRICK to the Brussels sprouts no one is doing is peeling off the leaves and wilting them in melted butter so they are very tender. The salmon is baked slowly but should be served very rare.

Makes 1 serving

1 cup Brussels sprouts
   (about 6 medium to large sprouts)
2 Tbsp. butter
1 Tbsp. water
1 to 2 Tbsp. balsamic vinegar
Salt and black pepper, to taste
1 skin-on salmon fillet (7 to 8 oz.)
1 Tbsp. white truffle oil
½ tsp. fleur de sel
½ tsp. coarse ground black pepper
1½ tsp. chopped fresh chives
Mashed Potatoes
   (see recipe in Vegetables chapter)

Heat oven to 250°F.

Trim about ¼ inch off stem end of each Brussels sprout. Remove and discard the tough or marred exterior leaves. Peel away the remaining leaves on each sprout; set aside. Discard cores.

Melt butter with water in large sauté pan. Add Brussels sprout leaves; cook until they start to wilt, stirring frequently. Add balsamic vinegar to taste. Season with salt and pepper. Cover to keep warm.

Bake fish in shallow ovenproof dish 12 to 14 min. or until fish flakes easily with fork but is still rare. Remove from oven; carefully remove and discard skin and dark meat.

Place fish on center of plate; sprinkle with truffle oil, fleur de sel, black pepper and chives. Spoon Brussels sprouts onto one side of salmon, and hot Mashed Potatoes onto other side.

DEVILED CRAB

THERE USED TO BE a fishmonger at 79th Street and Lexington Avenue called Rosedale, and the owner, Bob Neuman, gave me the recipe for their deviled crab a long time ago and I misplaced it. His successor, Dorian Mecir, took over the business and moved it to 83rd Street and First Avenue, and she was kind enough to give it to me a second time. The seasonings for the crab are just right.

Makes 1 serving

¾ cup lump crabmeat, picked over to remove
   cartilage and shell fragments, well drained
1 Tbsp. butter, softened
1 Tbsp. heavy cream
1 tsp. Worcestershire sauce
1 tsp. grated onion
¼ tsp. salt
⅛ tsp. ground black pepper
Zest of 1 lemon
1½ Tbsp. bread crumbs
¼ tsp. paprika
½ Tbsp. cold butter, cubed
Chopped fresh chives (for garnish)

Heat oven to 425°F.

Combine crabmeat, softened butter, cream, Worcestershire sauce, onion, salt, pepper and lemon zest. Spoon into gratin dish.

Top with bread crumbs, paprika and cubed cold butter.

Bake 12 min. or until heated through. Garnish with chives.

TUNA WITH AVOCADO RISOTTO AND KAFFIR LIME SAUCE

WHEN I'M WORKING in Mexico City, I very often stay at the Four Seasons, and this is my favorite dish there.

Makes 4 servings

Kaffir Sauce
2 Tbsp. olive oil
½ cup finely chopped shallots
2 garlic cloves, finely chopped
1 cup dry white wine
½ cup heavy cream
1 Meyer lemon, cut into ½-inch-thick slices
2 kaffir lime leaves
Salt and pepper, to taste

Tuna
¹/₃ cup paprika
¹/₃ cup chipotle chile pepper powder
1 Tbsp. ground cumin
1 Tbsp. salt
3 Tbsp. butter
3 Tbsp. olive oil
4 tuna medallions (6 oz. each),
*   sinew parts scraped away with a spoon*
*   and reserved for another use*
1 Tbsp. finely chopped lemon zest

Risotto
3 Tbsp. butter, divided use
2 Tbsp. olive oil
1 large shallot, finely chopped
1¼ cups Arborio rice
1 cup dry white wine
6 to 8 cups chicken stock or broth
*   (purchased or homemade), very hot*
1¼ cups finely chopped avocados
⅓ cup grated Parmigiano-Reggiano
1 Tbsp. butter

Kaffir Sauce
Heat olive oil in small saucepan. Add shallots and garlic; sauté 3 min. Add wine; cook until reduced to about ¼ cup. Stir in cream; bring to boil. Add lemon slices and kaffir leaves; stir. Simmer 10 min. Strain sauce; discard strained solids. Season sauce with salt and pepper.

Tuna
Mix dry seasonings until blended; rub evenly onto tuna. Melt butter with oil in large skillet on medium-high heat. Add tuna; cook 30 sec. on each side or just until seared on both sides. Remove from heat; set aside.

Risotto

Melt 2 Tbsp. butter with olive oil in large saucepan. Add shallots; sauté 3 min. Add rice; cook and stir 1 min. or until rice is evenly coated with butter mixture. Stir in wine; cook until completely absorbed by rice. Start adding hot stock, about ½ cup at the time. The rice should absorb the liquid as slowly as possible. Continue adding the rest of the stock until rice is tender.

Add avocados, cheese and remaining 1 Tbsp. butter; stir gently until butter is melted.

Assembly

For each serving, spoon 1 Tbsp. Kaffir Sauce onto center of shallow soup plate; top with ¼ of the Risotto. Cut 1 tuna medallion into diagonal slices; arrange over risotto. Drizzle with 2 tsp. of the remaining Kaffir Sauce.

TIPS

• *Garnish plated dish with chopped fresh chives or parsley.*

• *Rice can be cooked ahead of time. Let stand at room temperature up to 1½ hours. When ready to serve, gently stir avocados and cheese into rice; cook over low heat until heated through, stirring frequently. Use as directed.*

• *To get a head start, the risotto can be partially cooked ahead of time. Cook as directed in recipe, stopping when 1 to 1½ cups of the chicken stock is left. (Rice will not be done.) Cool risotto, then refrigerate. When ready to serve, heat remaining chicken stock, then use to finish cooking risotto as directed.*

FAIRVIEW JUMBO LUMP CRAB CAKES WITH PICKLED OKRA AIOLI

THE SECRET of good crab cakes is having lots of crab in large pieces that will hold together during in the cooking process, and having it very well-seasoned. These fulfill both those criteria. You can serve a variety of different sauces with them, like Chile-Mayo, but I like this aioli. This recipe was given to me by the chef at the Washington-Duke Inn in North Carolina, Jason Cunningham.

Makes 4 servings as a main course,
8 as a first course

Pickled Okra Aioli
½ cup whole peeled garlic cloves
Vegetable oil to cover
1¼ cups mayonnaise, preferably Lesieur
1 Tbsp. white wine vinegar
1 Tbsp. chopped fresh parsley
1 tsp. chopped fresh thyme
¼ cup seeded and diced pickled okra
¼ tsp Tabasco
Salt and pepper to taste

Crab cakes
1 lb. fresh jumbo lump crab meat
1 large egg
¼ cup mayonnaise
1 Tbsp. fresh lemon juice
1 tsp. Dijon mustard
½ tsp. Old Bay Seasoning
Dash Tabasco sauce
1 Tbsp. chopped fresh chives
Salt and pepper, to taste
½ cup finely ground fresh bread crumbs
Olive oil

Pickled Okra Aioli
Place garlic cloves in a small saucepan. Cover with vegetable oil and place on stove over medium heat and cook until the cloves begin to turn golden brown. Remove from heat and allow to cool completely.

Drain garlic and combine with mayonnaise and vinegar in a food processor. Blend until smooth. Transfer to a small mixing bowl and whisk in the remaining ingredients until well combined. Adjust seasoning to taste.

Recipe continues on page 108

Recipe continued from page 106

Refrigerate sauce 4 to 6 hours before serving to allow flavors to bloom. Store in refrigerator up to 14 days.

Crab cakes
Pick through crabmeat for any random shells, being careful to not break up the meat too much.

Mix all remaining ingredients except bread crumbs and oil in medium bowl until blended. Add crab meat; stir gently until evenly coated. Add bread crumbs; mix well. Shape into 8 large crab cakes.

Place in freezer for 20 minutes, then refrigerate 1 hour so mixture is very firm.

Heat oven to 350°F.

Heat large ovenproof sauté pan over medium to medium-high heat.

Add enough olive oil to pan to evenly coat bottom. Add crab cakes; cook 1 to 2 min. on each side or until bottoms are golden brown. Place pan in oven.

Bake 7 to 8 min. or until heated through.

TIP
• *Check the crab mixture by making a small sample cake. If the mixture is too dry, add a little more mayonnaise. Or if the crab mixture is too moist, add a little more bread crumbs.*

SEA SCALLOPS WRAPPED IN BACON WITH MUSSELS SAUCE

THIS VARIATION uses large sea scallops with bacon around them. If you add some leeks and mushrooms, even button mushrooms, to the plate, that makes up for the sea scallops not being as interesting to taste as those from Nantucket Bay.

Makes 6 main-course servings

Mussels Sauce (page 94)

Vegetables
2 leeks
2 to 3 Tbsp. vegetable oil
30 fresh button mushrooms, sliced

Scallops
30 thin bacon slices
30 sea scallops, thick white nerves removed
½ cup chopped fresh chives (for garnish)
Salt and pepper, to taste

Vegetables
Remove green parts and roots from leeks; discard. Cut leek whites into 2-inch-long julienne; soak in cold water 5 min. to clean. Drain leeks. Add to salted boiling water in saucepan; cook 6 to 8 min. or until softened. Drain leeks; place in medium bowl.

Heat oil in large skillet over medium heat. Add mushrooms; sauté until tender and lightly browned. Add to leeks; mix well.

Scallops
Heat oven to 350°F. Trim bacon to length just long enough to wrap around circumference of each scallop. Wrap scallops with bacon, leaving flat sides of scallops unwrapped; secure with wooden toothpicks broken in half (so that the bacon can touch the skillet. Season scallops with salt and pepper. Cook scallops, in batches if necessary, in skillet for several minutes or until they start to brown; turn. (The toothpicks will only allow you to brown from top to bottom.) Cook 1 to 2 min. or until heated through. Transfer to single layer in baking pan. Bake 5 min. or until scallops are opaque and bacon is done.

Assembly
Spoon ½ cup Vegetables onto center of each 6 plates; top with 5 Scallops. Surround with Mussels Sauce. Garnish with chives.

TIP
• *If serving as a first course, recipe makes 10 to 12 servings.*

PANKO-CRUSTED SALMON WITH CASHEWS AND HONEY MUSTARD

I DISCOVERED this at the most famous restaurant in Panama City, Maito, where the chef, Mario Castrellon, was kind enough to share the recipe. The coating and the crust simply make the salmon come alive. The crust proportions here yield enough to keep on hand for more meals.

Makes 6 servings

6 portions salmon, 6-ounce fillets or 8-ounce steaks

Glaze
2 Tbsp. regular yellow mustard
1 Tbsp. Dijon mustard
1 Tbsp. chopped fresh rosemary
1 cup honey

Crust
½ pound butter
½ pound panko
2 ounces cashews, powdered
  (use a food processor)
Zest of 1 orange
Zest of 1 lemon
6 portions salmon, 6 to 8 ounces each
Salt

Heat oven to 350 degrees.

Glaze
Combine regular and Dijon mustard with rosemary and honey and mix well.

Crust
Melt butter and mix with panko, cashews and orange and lemon zest.

Assembly
Lightly season salmon with salt. Spread just enough of the glaze over the top side of each fillet or steak to cover. Spread a thick layer of the panko mixture over the glaze.

Bake 4 to 5 minutes, then transfer to broiler and cook until crust is golden brown and fish is done (thin-blade knife inserted into the thickest part will go in easily). Drizzle with a little more of the glaze and serve.

POULTRY

CHICKEN HASH

THIS RECIPE is a version of the chicken hash at the '21' Club, which I found was easy to improve upon. The first problem was getting the chicken right, and my technique of slow roasting is the best I've found (page 121). The hash is finished with a cheese crust in gratin dishes under the broiler, and the quality of the Gruyere and the Parmigiano-Reggiano makes a vast difference in the flavor. Serve this with Purée of Peas with Mint and Cilantro (page 160).

Makes 4 servings

3 Tbsp. butter
¼ cup finely chopped onion
3 Tbsp. flour
2 cups whole milk
4 cups bite-size cooked chicken pieces,
  preferably white meat
1 tsp. salt, or to taste
½ tsp. white pepper, or to taste
1½ cups shredded Gruyère, Comte if possible
1 cup grated Parmigiano-Reggiano

Melt butter in medium saucepan over medium-low heat. Add onions; sauté over low heat 5 minutes or until translucent. Add flour; stir until blended. Cook over medium heat 5 minutes or until mixture turns a light, golden sandy color. Meanwhile, heat milk in separate pan until just about to boil. (Be careful not to let it come to a boil or it will spill over.)

Add hot milk, ½ cup at a time, to roux, whisking after each addition until well blended. Bring to a simmer; cook 8 minutes, stirring constantly. Stir in chicken, salt and pepper; return to a simmer.

Heat broiler. Spoon chicken mixture into 4 gratin dishes; top with cheeses. Broil until cheeses are melted.

CHICKEN MEATBALLS WITH PUMMAROLA/TOMATO SAUCE

THE CHICKEN MEATBALLS at Sistina on the Upper East Side are top of the line, flavored with sun-dried tomatoes, capers and rosemary. The owner, Giuseppe Bruno, was kind enough to share the recipe, which I've rejiggered slightly. Be sure to use a pan that will allow the meatballs to be completely covered in sauce as they finish cooking.

Makes 4 to 6 servings

Pummarola/Tomato Sauce
2 Tbsp. olive oil
1 Spanish onion, chopped
1 celery stalk, chopped
1 carrot, chopped
2 large garlic cloves, finely chopped
1 qt. chicken stock
1 28-oz. can crushed tomatoes
10 fresh parsley sprigs
8 large fresh basil leaves
2 Tbsp. butter
Salt and pepper, to taste

Meatballs
½ cup fresh bread crumbs
¾ cup milk
1½ lbs. ground chicken breast
2 cup grated Parmesan cheese
1 Tbsp. chopped fresh parsley
2 Tbsp. chopped sun-dried tomatoes
1 tsp. chopped capers
2 garlic cloves, minced
2 tsp. chopped fresh rosemary
Salt and pepper to taste
1 egg
1 cup flour
2 Tbsp. Butter
2 Tbsp. olive oil
Cooked, peeled fava beans (for garnish)
Shaved Parmigiano-Reggiano (for garnish)

Pummarola/Tomato Sauce
Heat oil in Dutch oven or large saucepan. Add onions, celery, carrots and garlic; sauté 5 min. or until vegetables start to soften. Add chicken stock and cook until reduced by 25 percent. Add tomatoes, parsley and basil; mix well. Cover; simmer over low heat 1 hour, uncovering and gently shaking pan every 20

to 30 minutes to prevent ingredients from sticking to bottom of pan. Press sauce through a food mill; return to pan. Add butter; cook until butter is melted and sauce is reduced to desired consistency, stirring frequently. Season with salt and pepper. Cool slightly.

Meatballs

While sauce cooks, soak bread crumbs in milk in medium bowl 1 minute. Place in strainer lined with cheesecloth; drain. Discard milk. Squeeze bread crumbs dry. Return to bowl. Add chicken, cheese, parsley, sun-dried tomatoes, capers, garlic, rosemary, salt, pepper and egg; mix just until blended. Shape into 1½-inch balls. (If the mixture is too wet/soft, freeze until you can handle the meat easily.) Roll in flour until evenly coated; gently shake off excess flour.

Melt butter with oil in medium skillet over medium heat. Add meatballs, a few at a time without crowding; cook until evenly browned, turning occasionally. Cover to keep warm.

Add Meatballs to Pummarola/Tomato Sauce; bring to a simmer. Cook 15 minutes or until done (165°F), stirring occasionally. Serve garnished with fava beans and Parmigiano.

TIPS

• *Serve with your choice of hot cooked pasta.*

• *For best results, use a pan that is large enough to allow the meatballs to be completely covered with the sauce as they cook.*

• *Substitute canned whole tomatoes for the canned crushed tomatoes. Drain tomatoes, then crush by hand before using as directed.*

CHICKEN POTPIE

GLORIA CICCARONE-NEHLS, who was the chef at the Huntington Hotel in San Francisco for many years, made what I always thought was the best chicken potpie in the world. She was kind enough to share the recipe with me, and I was presumptuous enough to rejigger it slightly. This starts with great chicken — the best comes from my slow-cooked chicken recipe (page 121) — but the sauce is also important. There's no Campbell's; it's a combination of homemade stock and a dry-sherry reduction. (When pressed, you can use store-bought stock.) The "crust" is made from Dufour puff pastry, which is head and shoulders above other brands, but use what you can find. It's better to overcook than undercook the dough.

Makes 4 servings

1 baking potato, peeled
1 large carrot,
    cut into ¼-inch-thick slices
12 small pearl onions, peeled
6 Tbsp. Butter
5 Tbsp. flour
1 cup dry sherry
¾ cup dry white wine
1½ qt. (6 cups) chicken stock or broth
    (purchased or homemade)
6 to 8 flat parsley leaves
5 sprigs fresh thyme
3 sage leaves, rough-chopped
¾ cup heavy cream
6 cups bite-size cooked chicken breast
½ cup frozen peas, thawed
1 pkg. (14 oz.) Dufour puff pastry
    (1 sheet), thawed
1 egg, beaten

Use small melon baller to scoop balls from potato, or cut the potato into medium dice. Place in large saucepan. Add enough water to cover pieces; bring to boil. Cook 8 to 10 min. or until almost cooked through. Meanwhile, cook carrots and onions in separate pans of boiling water just until almost cooked through. Drain all the vegetables well and set aside.

Heat oven to 350°F.

Melt butter in medium ovenproof saucepan over medium heat. Stir in flour; cook 2

minutes, stirring constantly. Place in oven. Bake 10 minutes. Remove from oven; set aside.

Increase oven temperature to 375°F.

Bring sherry and wine to boil in separate medium saucepan; cook until reduced by half. Add chicken stock; cook until reduced by half. (You should have about 3 cups.) Add parsley, thyme and sage; stir. Return just to boil. Add roux; cook until thickened, stirring constantly. Stir in cream until it starts to thicken. Remove from heat. Remove and discard thyme sprigs.

Divide chicken equally among 4 (2 ½-cup/5-by 2-inch) ramekins. Top each portion with equal amounts of vegetables, then sauce.

Roll out pastry sheet on lightly floured surface to ⅛-inch thickness; cut into 4 rounds, each about ½ inch larger than tops of ramekins. Place pastry over ramekins; press edges to tops of ramekins to seal. Brush with egg. Place ramekins on baking sheet.

Bake 15 to 20 minutes or until crusts are golden brown, then serve.

CHICKEN PARMA

PARMA RESTAURANT was kind enough to also share this recipe, which is one of my favorites for chicken. Carefully skinning and trimming the chicken breast makes a big difference.

Makes 4 servings

4 chicken breasts (6 to 8 oz. each),
  skinned, trimmed and pounded
  to ¼-inch thickness
Salt and pepper
2 eggs
1½ cups dry bread crumbs
1 cup grated Parmigiano-Reggiano
3 Tbsp. butter
2 Tbsp. canola oil
1 cup dry white wine
¼ cup lemon juice
Chopped fresh parsley or chopped chives
  (for garnish)

Season chicken with salt and pepper. Whisk eggs in shallow dish. Combine bread crumbs and cheese in separate shallow dish.

Dip chicken, 1 breast at a time, in eggs; gently shake off excess egg (while holding over dish). Dip in bread crumb mixture, turning to evenly coat both sides of each breast; shake gently to remove excess crumbs before placing in single layer on plate. Melt butter with oil in medium skillet over medium heat, being careful to not burn the butter. Add chicken; cook 1 to 2 minutes on each side or until evenly browned on both sides. Remove chicken from skillet, reserving drippings in skillet; set chicken aside. Add wine and lemon juice to drippings in skillet; bring to boil. Simmer over medium-low heat until liquid is reduced by half. Return chicken to skillet; cook 1 to 2 minutes or until heated through and done (165°F).

Plate chicken to serve family style. Or, place on individual serving plates. Spoon sauce from skillet over chicken. Garnish with chopped parsley or chopped chives.

SLOW-COOKED CHICKEN

THIS RECIPE IS BASICALLY for chicken in a pot, but I've discovered it is the best way to cook chicken you want to use in another dish. The slow cooking makes the bird very tender. The vegetables are added to have the benefit of some stock left at the end of cooking.

Makes 3 to 4 servings

1 whole roasting chicken (3½ to 5 lbs.),
* innards removed and discarded*
2 tsp. kosher salt
¼ tsp. ground black pepper
2 Tbsp. vegetable oil
2 Tbsp. butter
2 stalks celery, medium dice
1 small onion, medium dice
2 Tbsp. coarsely chopped parsnips
4 garlic cloves, peeled, trimmed

Heat oven to 250°F. Adjust oven rack to lowest position. Cut the chicken's skin between the legs and the body. Season the chicken with salt and pepper.

Heat oil and butter in Dutch oven over medium heat. Add chicken and brown well on all sides. Add vegetables to pan. Cover pan tightly with aluminum foil, then with lid. Place in oven.

Bake 1 hour to 1 hour 50 minutes, or until chicken is done (165°F). (To test, insert the instant-read thermometer into the thickest part of breast and thigh.)

Transfer chicken to carving board; tent with foil. Let stand 20 minutes before carving and serving (discard the skin if you like. Meanwhile, strain chicken juices from pan through fine-mesh strainer; press on strained solids to remove as much liquid as possible. (You should have about ¾ cup strained broth.) Transfer broth to refrigerator and chill until fat congeals on the surface and can be removed. Reserve broth for another use.

FOUR SEASONS ROAST DUCK WITH CHERRY SAUCE

BEFORE the Four Seasons closed in the Seagram Building, I went for one last dinner of this famous duck and persuaded the headwaiter to get me the recipe. It is so simple that I think they stole it from the Chinese; it looks just like the hanging ducks you see on Mott Street. At the restaurant it's served plain; however I prefer it with my own cherry sauce. Every oven is different, so do check the duck early and often as it roasts.

Makes 2 servings

Duck
2 cups dark brown sugar
2 cups (16 ounces) soy sauce
1 small duck

Sauce
1 Tbsp. olive oil
4 medium shallots, minced (about ¹/₃ cup)
1½ cups dry white wine
½ cup dried cherries
2 cups chicken stock, homemade or purchased
¼ cup butter (½ stick), cut into pieces
1 Tbsp. Lambrusco vinegar
Salt and freshly ground black pepper to taste

Duck
Mix sugar and soy sauce in a medium bowl until sugar is completely dissolved. Set aside. Remove neck and giblets from duck and reserve for another use (like stock). Trim excess fat from cavity and discard or reserve for another use. Place duck in container just large enough to hold it and pour sugar-soy marinade over. Refrigerate 2½ days, turning once after 1½ days.

Preheat oven to 500 degrees. Prick duck skin all over. Place duck on a rack in a roasting pan pan and brown in the oven for 15 minutes. Reduce the oven setting to 275 degrees. Continue cooking, basting as you go, until the legs can be moved easily and clear juices are released from the meat when tested with a fork. Start testing after about 1½ hours. The duck may take up to 3 hours or more to cook depending on its size.

Sauce
Heat olive oil in medium skillet over medium-high heat. Add shallots; sauté 2 to 3 minutes, or until softened. Add wine and cherries and cook, stirring frequently, 5 minutes, or until thickened to syrup-like consistency. Add chicken stock; cook 5 to 8 minutes, or until sauce is thickened and reduced to about 2 cups. Add butter; whisk until melted. Remove from heat. Whisk in vinegar. Season with salt and pepper.

Remove the duck from the oven to a carving board and tent loosely with foil. Set sit about 10 minutes, then carve off the breast and legs from the carcass. Serve the meat with cherry sauce on the side.

ROAST CHICKEN ARQUA

THIS RECIPE CAME from Leo Pulito, the owner of the old Arqua in TriBeCa, and the chicken turns out wonderful just as they did it there. However, my secret is with the sauce. At the restaurant, they would carve the chicken and serve it with the sauce on top. I like to carve the chicken into slices and then spread the sauce on both sides of the meat, so it soaks up the flavor.

Makes 2 to 3 servings

Chicken
1 whole chicken (3 to 3½ lbs.)
2 tsp. coarse salt, divided use
2 tsp. coarsely ground black pepper, divided use
¼ lemon
3 sage leaves
1 sprig fresh rosemary
2 garlic cloves, mashed
3 Tbsp. vegetable oil

Sauce
3 to 4 Tbsp. vegetable oil
1 onion, coarsely chopped
2 celery stalks, coarsely chopped
3 garlic cloves, mashed
½ cup dry white wine
3 cups chicken stock or broth
   (purchased or homemade)
¼ cup butter
¼ cup flour
Salt and pepper, to taste

Chicken
Season inside of chicken with half each of the salt and pepper; fill cavity with lemon, sage, rosemary and garlic. Sprinkle remaining salt and pepper onto outside of chicken. Truss chicken to enclose all stuffing.

Heat oil in large skillet on medium heat. Add chicken, breast side down; cook until evenly browned on both sides, turning as needed.

Sauce
Heat oil in medium skillet on medium heat. Add vegetables and garlic; cook until vegetables are translucent and slightly softened.

Assembly

Heat oven to 425°F. Place chicken and cooked vegetables in roasting pan. Add wine, chicken stock and water.

Bake 1 hour or until chicken is done (165°F), turning after 30 min. Remove chicken from pan; cover with foil. Set aside.

Strain vegetable mixture, reserving liquid and pressing cooked vegetables to remove as much liquid as possible. Discard strained solids. (If you have time, place the strained liquid mixture in the freezer long enough to solidify the fat, 30 to 45 minutes, then remove and discard the fat.) You should have 3 cups; if not, cook until reduced.

Melt butter in medium saucepan on medium heat. Add flour; cook and stir 1 minute. Add reserved strained vegetable liquid; cook until sauce is thickened, stirring constantly. Season with salt and pepper.

Carve the chicken. Dredge the pieces in the sauce to coat thoroughly and serve.

TIP
• *If serving later, reheat the chicken in 300°F oven 10 to 15 minutes. or until heated through. Meanwhile, heat the sauce in saucepan just until warmed.*

GUINEA HEN

IN COOKING ALL SORTS of fowl, the trick is having the audacity to cook the legs and breast separately. Because of their muscular structure, the legs cook very differently and take longer than the breasts. This recipe was given to me by Giuseppe Bruno, the owner of Sistina in New York City.

Makes 2 servings

2 guinea fowl
10 peppercorns
6 sprigs fresh thyme
1 bay leaf
Vegetable oil
1 lemon, cut in half
12 large parsley sprigs
2 cloves garlic
Salt and pepper, to taste

Cut legs from fowl. Place legs in saucepan. Add peppercorns, thyme, bay leaf and enough oil to completely cover legs. Bring to boil; simmer on medium-low heat 1½ hours or until legs are done (165°F) and very tender. Meanwhile, refrigerate remaining fowl until ready to use.

Remove cooked legs from oil mixture; discard oil mixture. Add legs to skillet; cook on medium heat until evenly browned, turning occasionally.

Meanwhile, heat oven to 375°F. Stuff each guinea breast with 1 lemon half, 6 parsley sprigs and 1 garlic clove. Season with salt and pepper. Place in roasting pan. Bake until done (165°F).

Serve fowl legs with the stuffed breasts and your favorite cooked vegetables.

CHEATER'S DUCK CONFIT

GALLONS OF DUCK FAT are usually needed to confit the legs, but if you want to get the supremely tender meat without the excess and expense you can try this technique developed by one of my collaborators, Regina Schrambling: Salt-cure the legs overnight, then slowly bake them in a tightly covered pan so they stew in their own fat and juices. For the recipes in this book you will not need the skin, but if you choose to serve these like "real" confit, just run the legs under the broiler or sear them in a skillet to crisp the skin.

Makes 8 legs, 4 to 8 servings

8 duck legs (Pekin, not moulard)
¼ cup kosher salt
1 teaspoon herbes de Provence
1 teaspoon juniper berries, crushed
1 teaspoon ground allspice
1 teaspoon coarsely ground black pepper
1 bay leaf
8 large garlic cloves, peeled

Twenty-hour hours ahead, rub the legs all over with a mixture of the salt, herbes de Provence, juniper berries, allspice and pepper. Place in a glass dish large enough to hold them all in a single layer, cover with plastic wrap and refrigerate.

Next day, heat the oven to 300 degrees. Carefully wipe the legs with paper towels to remove all the salt. Place skin side up in a baking dish just large enough to hold them all in a single layer. Add the bay leaf to the pan and arrange the garlic cloves among the legs. Cover tightly with foil and bake 2½ to 3 hours, until the meat is extremely tender when pierced with a skewer.

PERFECT ROAST TURKEY

ROASTING THE TURKEY in two parts, with the legs cooked in confit, solves the problem of having to overcook the breast to get the dark meat done. For a richer stock, add extra turkey necks for the collagen. For a darker gravy, brown the bones in the oven at 350 degrees before making the stock. You can make the legs and the stock in advance.

Makes 10 to 12 servings

1 whole turkey, 12 to 15 pounds
1 onion, diced
2 carrots, diced
2 stalks celery, diced
2 parsnips, peeled and diced
3 to 4 Tbsp. olive oil
1 bay leaf
1 Tbsp. plus 2 Tbsp. soy sauce
1 Tbsp Marmite
Salt and freshly ground black pepper to taste
Duck or goose fat to cover legs
¼ cup butter
¼ cup flour

Have the butcher carve the breasts off the bones, leaving the skin on, and remove the wings, legs and thighs.

Stock
Brown the wings and carcass (and extra necks, if using) in the oven at 350 degrees. Transfer to a large stockpot. Toss the onion, carrots, celery and parsnips with the olive oil and bake until they take on color but are not browned. Transfer to the stockpot. Add the bay leaf along with 1 tablespoon of the soy sauce and the Marmite. Add water to cover. Bring to a boil, skim off the scum that surfaces and reduce the heat. Simmer until the stock is very rich. If you have time, refrigerate until you can remove the fat that surfaces. Strain, discarding solids, and reserve the liquid.

Confit
Heat oven to 300 degrees. Place the legs and thighs in a baking dish just large enough to hold them. Season with salt and pepper. Add melted duck or goose fat to cover. Add remaining soy sauce. Cover and roast on the lower rack of the oven until the meat is falling off the bones, about three hours.

After about one hour, season the breasts with salt and pepper. Using kitchen twine, tie the two parts together in seven or eight places with the non-skin sides flush against each other. Roast on the upper rack of the oven until a meat thermometer registers 150 degrees, about two hours.

Remove all the meat to a carving board. Strain off any cooking liquid and add to the reserved stock. Heat a large nonstick skillet and sear the breast on all sides to brown.

Return to the carving board, tent with aluminum foil and let rest while you make the gravy.

Gravy
Bring the reserved stock to a simmer. Melt the butter in a medium saucepan, then whisk in the flour. Cook a few minutes, whisking, then gradually add reserved stock. Cook, whisking, until gravy thickens to desired consistency. Season to taste with salt and pepper. Carve the turkey and serve with gravy.

TURKEY MEATBALLS WITH JERK BARBECUE SAUCE

I HAD THESE at a private club in Manhattan called Doubles, where the chef, Steve Mellina, was kind enough to share the recipe. The secret ingredient in the tangy sauce is Jamaican jerk seasoning, which you can buy in any good supermarket.

Makes 4 or more servings, depending on size of meatballs

Meatballs
1 lb. ground turkey (or you can use chicken)
1 cup panko
1 Tbsp. garlic powder
1 Tbsp. onion powder
2 tsp. salt
½ cup mayonnaise
2 Tbsp. Dijon mustard
2 Tbsp. ketchup
1 egg, beaten

Barbecue Sauce
1 qt. (4 cups) ketchup
2 cups apple juice
1 cup molasses
1 cup packed dark brown sugar
1 Tbsp. ground cumin
1 Tbsp. garlic powder
1 Tbsp. onion powder
1 Tbsp. smoked paprika
1 to 2 Tbsp. liquid smoke
1 tsp. jerk seasoning
Chopped fresh chives for garnish

Meatballs
Heat oven to 375°F.

Mix ingredients just until blended. Shape into desired-size meatballs.

Place on rimmed baking sheet sprayed with cooking spray.

Bake 10 to 15 min. or until done (165°F).

Barbecue Sauce
Bring ingredients to boil in saucepan on medium heat, stirring frequently.

Toss meatballs with sauce just before serving. Garnish with chives.

CHICKEN PARMIGIANA

IT SOUNDS CRAZY, but the most important part of making chicken Parmigiana is being sure all the skin and sinews are trimmed from the meat before you start, so every bite is totally tender. Using Muenster cheese instead of the traditional mozzarella is a vast improvement because it melts just as well but has more taste — mozzarella is a nice idea, but it's bland. Parmigiano-Reggiano versus cheaper grana padano makes a big difference as well. This version is adapted from the Parma restaurant at 80th Street and Third Avenue in New York.

Makes 4 servings

4 boneless, skinless chicken breasts
    (6 to 8 oz. each), trimmed of sinews,
    pounded to 1/8-inch thickness
Salt and pepper, to taste
1 Tbsp. Flour
2 eggs, beaten
¾ cup plain dry bread crumbs
¼ cup butter
¼ cup canola oil
1 cup Pummarola/Tomato Sauce
8 slices Muenster cheese,
    cut into 1-inch-wide strips
1¼ cups grated Parmigiano-Reggiano

Heat broiler.

Season chicken with salt and pepper. Dip 1 breast at a time in flour. Gently shake off excess flour, then repeat to coat chicken with eggs and bread crumbs, gently shaking chicken after coating with each ingredient.

Melt butter with oil in large skillet over medium heat. Add chicken; cook 2 to 3 minutes on each side or until evenly browned on both sides. Place in single layer in baking dish; cover with Pummarola/Tomato Sauce. Top with Muenster cheese, leaving $1/8$-inch space between cheese strips. Sprinkle with Parmigiano.

Broil, about 6 inches from heat, 2 to 3 minutes, or until chicken is done, Muenster cheese is melted and Parmigiano is starting to turn golden.

Line in front of the Butcher Shop
Etching on laid paper • Édouard Manet, Paris 1870–71
Rogers Fund, 1921

MEAT

TOP-SECRET STEAK TARTARE

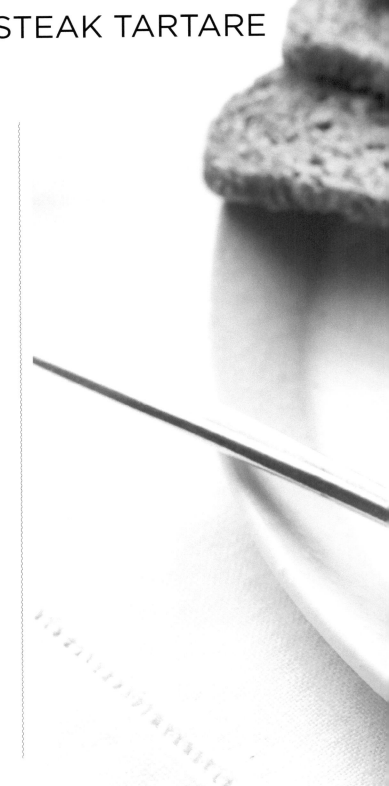

I CAN'T REVEAL the source of this excellent version of the classic. Let's just say "an old friend in Cincinnati." The meat should be chopped or ground right before you make this so it keeps its color.

Makes 2 to 3 servings

1 pound filet mignon or sirloin,
*   freshly ground or finely chopped*
1 egg yolk
1 Tbsp. Dijon mustard
1 Tbsp. chopped cornichons
1½ Tbsp. chopped parsley
6 Tbsp. ketchup
1½ Tbsp. chopped shallots
1 tsp. Worcestershire sauce
1 tsp. Tabasco sauce
1 Tbsp. extra-virgin olive oil
1½ tsp. each salt and pepper

Combine all ingredients and mix well. Serve with toast points.

BARBECUED BABYBACK RIBS

UNTIL A FEW YEARS AGO there was a barbecue restaurant on Park Avenue South; it didn't make it. One day I noticed that they were having their chief barbecue chef give one day's worth of lessons. He was a retired state policeman who had won every award for his barbecue recipes. Two of them I thought were worth taking down, these babyback ribs and the smoked pulled pork that follows. You really can't do these in a Weber; you need a ceramic smoker. If you're willing to put in the time — and it does take a lot of time — these are both spectacular. The dry rub and barbecue sauce subrecipes here yield enough for several batches of ribs.

Makes 4 servings

1¾ lb. (794 g) babyback ribs

Dry Rub
2 cups packed dark brown sugar
½ cup kosher salt
½ cup turbinado sugar
¼ cup smoked paprika
1 Tbsp. black pepper
1 Tbsp. white pepper
1 Tbsp. onion powder
1 Tbsp. Garlic powder
1 tsp. ancho chile powder
1 tsp. ground cumin
1 tsp. ground celery seed
½ tsp. cayenne
Yellow mustard, for rubbing

Apple-Bourbon BBQ Sauce
2 Tbsp. Butter
¾ cup grated apple
¼ cup finely chopped onion
3 Tbsp. bourbon
¼ tsp. kosher salt
¼ tsp. cayenne
¼ tsp. cinnamon
¼ tsp. ground cumin
2 cups ketchup
½ cup apple cider vinegar
½ cup Dr Pepper
½ cup packed dark brown sugar
⅓ cup maple syrup
1 Tbsp. molasses
1 Tbsp. Worcestershire sauce

Dry Rub
Mix all ingredients except mustard until well blended. Coat meaty sides of ribs with mustard, then enough of the dry rub to evenly coat meat. Refrigerate several hours.

Apple-Bourbon BBQ Sauce.
Melt butter in medium saucepan over medium heat. Add apples, onions, bourbon, salt, cayenne, cinnamon and cumin; cook 10 min., stirring frequently. Meanwhile, cook remaining ingredients in separate saucepan over medium heat 10 min., stirring frequently. Mix all ingredients; strain. Cool.

Heat smoker to 200°F to 220°F. Place ribs on rack in smoker; cook 2 hours. Remove from smoker; dust with additional Dry Rub. Wrap ribs with foil. Return to smoker. Cook additional 2 to 2½ hours or until ribs are tender and meat can easily be pulled away from bones. Remove and discard the foil. Heat grill or broiler. Brush ribs with Apple-Bourbon BBQ Sauce. Grill or broil just until glaze starts to caramelize.

TIPS
• *To save time, you can prepare this recipe using Blues Hog Barbecue Sauce (see Pantry).*

• *The Apple-Bourbon BBQ Sauce can be prepared ahead of time. Refrigerate up to 2 weeks before using as directed.*

• *The ribs can be prepared ahead of time. Smoke and grill (or broil) as directed. Cool, then wrap tightly and refrigerate up to 2 days. Reheat in 250°F oven just before serving.*

BRAISED SHORT RIBS WITH MUSTARD

GIUSEPPE BRUNO, who owns Sistina and Caravaggio in New York, was nice enough to give me his braised short rib recipe. I copied it down and cooked the short ribs several times. On another visit I asked him to confirm that the recipe was right and he said it was a little off. To me, however, they are equally good. If you're cooking this for a group in wintertime — and can find enough people who still eat meat — this is a spectacular dish. Mustard and balsamic white vinegar produce great flavor, and long, slow cooking ends in meat so tender you could eat it with a spoon. This is best made in advance (see Tips at right).

Makes 4 to 6 servings

5 sprigs fresh thyme
5 cloves garlic, crushed
3 to 5 Tbsp. olive oil
3½ lb. short ribs, cut lengthwise in half, boned and well trimmed
Salt and pepper, to taste
5 cups thinly sliced Vidalia onions
½ bottle dry red wine (about 2 cups)
1 cup white balsamic vinegar
3 Tbsp. brown sugar
1 cup veal stock (purchased or homemade)
1 cup beef stock (purchased or homemade)
3 Tbsp. Dijon mustard
Finely chopped fresh parsley or chives (for garnish)

Combine thyme, garlic and oil and pour evenly over ribs in container just large enough to fit them. Turn to coat well. Let stand at room temperature 3 hours, then refrigerate 7 to 10 hours. Place ribs in strainer placed over a bowl; drain 15 min., reserving about ¼ cup (you can reuse the remaining oil in another recipe). Discard thyme and garlic.

Cut ribs into 2½- to 3-inch pieces. Season with salt and pepper. Add ribs, in batches if necessary, to large skillet; cook 5 min. or until evenly browned, turning occasionally. Remove ribs from skillet; set aside. Add 2 Tbsp. or more of the reserved oil to skillet plus onions (in batches if necessary); cook until onions are soft and deep brown in color but not caramelized, stirring frequently to keep from burning and adding more oil if needed. Place ribs in Dutch oven; top with onions. Combine wine, vinegar and sugar; pour over ribs and onions. Cook 30 to 40 min. or until liquid is reduced by half. Add stocks and mustard; mix well. Pour over ribs.

Bake, uncovered, in 400°F oven 2 hours or until ribs are very tender. Plate the ribs. Garnish with chopped parsley or chives.

TIPS

• *If not serving right away, cool the ribs and then refrigerate the ribs in the Dutch oven overnight. The fat will then congeal on the surface. When ready to serve, just remove the congealed fat, including from between the ribs, then reheat the meat in a 275°F oven 15 to 20 min. or until heated through. Plate the ribs, then garnish as directed.*

• *An inexpensive olive oil is fine for this recipe because you need a lot. Homemade veal and beef stocks are best, but storebought is fine (Citarella's are commendable).*

ROASTED RACK OF LAMB

THIS RECIPE IS INSPIRED by one at Lenôtre in Paris, but I came up with the technique of separating the rack from the chops so you don't eat such a humongous amount of fat or have to wrestle with the bones. (Have the butcher do this if you prefer; he or she can also de-fat the meat and crack the ribs for the stock.) By cooking the loin independently you're able to get the meat to just the right doneness, and by using the bones to make stock before cooking the eye of lamb you can prepare the very tasty sauce in advance. I'm not sure why everyone doesn't do this. Good-quality balsamic vinegar is essential; for best results use Elsa or Ritrova from Modena.

Makes 2 servings

1 rack of lamb (about 8 ribs)
¼ cup canola oil, divided use
1 Tbsp. Butter
200 g onions (about 1 medium onion),
  medium dice
200g carrots (about 2 large carrots), medium dice
1 celery stalk (30 g), medium dice
20 fresh parsley stems
1 cup red wine

2 cups plus ½ cup chicken stock or broth
  (purchased or homemade)
Salt and pepper, to taste
10 fresh thyme sprigs
2 Tbsp. aged balsamic vinegar
1 each scant tsp. cornstarch and water,
  or more if needed if you want a thicker sauce
Chopped parsley or chives for garnish

Remove bones and fat from lamb; separate bones, fat and trimmings from eye of lamb rack. Discard fat. Sauté bones and trimmings in 3 Tbsp. hot oil in large skillet until evenly browned. Remove bones and trimmings from skillet; reserve for later use. Discard oil from skillet.

Melt butter in same skillet. Add onions, carrots and celery; sauté until evenly browned, adding more butter if necessary. (Stir constantly when cooking to prevent vegetables from burning, reducing the heat, if necessary.) Add parsley, then browned bones. Cook 3 min., stirring constantly. Stir in wine; cook until liquid is reduced by half.

Stir in 2 cups of the chicken stock. Season with salt and pepper. Simmer 1 hour, adding more water if necessary to keep ingredients covered with liquid. Remove from heat. Pour through strainer into saucepan; press strained solids with back of ladle or wooden spoon to remove as much liquid as possible. Discard strained solids.

Add thyme to stained liquid; simmer 10 min. until slightly reduced. If more sauce is desired, add about 1 cup additional chicken stock or water, then bring to boil. Reduce sauce to a slow simmer, then stir in balsamic vinegar. Place in refrigerator until fat comes to the surface, then skim off.

Return sauce to a simmer. Add the remaining ½ cup chicken stock. Mix cornstarch and water; whisk into sauce. Simmer 5 min. or until slightly thickened. Reserve until ready to serve.

Heat oven to 400°F. Season lamb with salt and pepper. Heat remaining 1 Tbsp. oil in large skillet. When bubbles subside, add lamb; cook until evenly browned, turning as needed. Transfer lamb to roasting pan; drizzle with oil from bottom of skillet.

Roast 5 to 8 min. or to medium-rare doneness (150°F to 155°F). Remove from oven. Let stand 10 to 15 min. before cutting into portions to serve. Plate sauce; top with meat. Garnish with parsley or chives.

SMOKED BARBECUE PULLED PORK

THIS IS ALSO from the prize-winning barbecue chef at the now-gone restaurant on Park Avenue South. Like the babyback ribs, this pork requires a serious investment of time but is well worth it. The pork butt needs to be injected with a sweet sauce, then treated with a spicy dry rub, then smoked for 16 hours or more before being sauced and pulled into shreds. Because it is a lot of effort, you should make this large amount. It is best if cooked in a smoker, although you can try this recipe in a low oven. The rub is good for more than one batch of pork.

Makes 6 to 8 servings

Meat
2 pork butts, 5 to 6 pounds each, fat trimmed

Injector Sauce
¾ cup apple juice
½ cup water
½ cup sugar
¼ cup salt
2 Tbsp. Worcestershire sauce

Dry Rub
Yellow mustard (enough to coat meat)
2 cups packed dark brown sugar
½ cup kosher salt
½ cup raw cane sugar
¼ cup smoked paprika
1 Tbsp. black pepper
1 Tbsp. white pepper
1 Tbsp. onion powder
1 Tbsp. garlic powder
1 tsp. ancho chile powder
1 tsp. ground cumin
1 tsp. ground celery seed
½ tsp. cayenne pepper

Baste and Sauce
1 cup apple juice

Apple-Bourbon BBQ Sauce
  (see BBQ Babyback Ribs recipe page 136)

Injector Sauce
Mix ingredients until blended; add to injector. Inject 3 to 4 oz. into meat, injecting all over meat until meat starts to refuse liquid. Pat meat dry. Let stand at least two hours.

Dry Rub
Rub meat with mustard. Mix remaining ingredients; press into meat, completely covering meat. Wrap tightly in plastic wrap. Refrigerate at least 2 hours.

Smoker Directions
Heat smoker to 200°F to 225°F. Unwrap meat; spray with apple juice. If using coals, push coals to one side of smoker; place meat on other side of smoker. Cook 12 to 16 hours, or until meat is very tender and falls off the bone (180°F to 190°F), adjusting vents and replenishing coals in smoker as necessary to regulate heat.

Grilling Directions
Heat grill to medium. Brush meat with Apple-Bourbon BBQ Sauce, using enough sauce to coat the ribs well. Grill 1 to 2 min. Remove from grill. Let stand 20 min. before pulling meat into shreds, removing any globs of fat. If desired, warm additional barbecue sauce to toss with the shredded meat.

TIPS
• *If Meat can be cooked in the oven instead of in the smoker. Heat oven to 225°F. Place meat, fat side up, on rack in roasting pan; spray with apple juice. Roast until very tender and falling off the bone. Transfer meat to grill. Brush with barbecue sauce, using enough to evenly coat meat. Grill and continue as directed.*

• *To save time, you can prepare this recipe using Blues Hog Barbecue Sauce (see Pantry).*

BRAISED PORK SHOULDER

THIS EASY RECIPE makes barbecue as good as you can find. You can make it in the wintertime, and you don't need a smoker. Serve it either in the sauce in which it cooks or with a good barbecue sauce, Blues Hogs or the one from previous recipe.

Serves 8 to 10

6 pounds pork shoulder, fat and bone removed, meat cut into quarters and tied if necessary

Marinade
1 Spanish onion, coarsely chopped
4 garlic cloves, chopped
4 sprigs thyme
4 sprigs rosemary
5 sage leaves
Equal parts grapeseed and canola oils
*   to cover meat*
Salt and freshly ground black pepper to taste

Cooking liquid
1½ cups white wine
2 cups chicken stock
2 cups veal stock
2 cups beef stock
4 sprigs thyme
4 sprigs rosemary
5 sage leaves

Place meat in a large bowl and strew the onion, garlic, thyme, rosemary and sage around it. Add oil to cover completely. Marinate at room temperature for three hours, then transfer to the refrigerator for six to seven hours.

Heat the oven to 375°F.

Remove meat from marinade, reserving the onion, garlic and herbs. Strain the oil and heat 2 tablespoons or more in a Dutch oven over medium to high heat. Season the meat all over with salt and pepper and sear on all sides until browned. Add wine, stock and reserved onion, garlic and herbs. Partially cover the pan and transfer to the oven. Bake 1½ to 3 hours, until the meat is falling-apart tender.

Remove the meat from the pot and transfer the cooking liquid to the refrigerator; when it cools, remove and discard the fat. Shred the meat, removing any sinew and fat. Before serving, reduce the cooking liquid to make a sauce, or combine the meat with barbecue sauce to serve on lightly toasted brioche rolls.

LAMB SHANKS

THIS IS A BLEND of various components of different recipes that I think ends up producing lamb shanks as good as any I've ever had. Anchovies in the tomato-and-veal stock cooking liquid contribute to the rich flavor. Puréed white beans make an excellent accompaniment.

Makes 8 servings

3 Tbsp. vegetable oil
8 meaty lamb shanks (½ lb. each),
*   well trimmed, shanks removed*
2 medium onions, medium dice
4 garlic cloves, medium dice
1 qt. dry red wine
6 fresh thyme sprigs
2 bay leaves
1 tsp. whole black peppercorns
6 stalks celery, medium dice
6 carrots, medium dice
6 anchovy fillets
1 qt. tomato purée
1 qt. veal stock (purchased or homemade)
Salt and black pepper, to taste
1 cup chopped fresh parsley

Heat oil in Dutch oven or large saucepan over medium heat. Add lamb; cook 5 min. on each side or until evenly browned on both sides. Remove from pan, reserving oil in pan; cover lamb to keep warm.

Add onions and garlic to pan; sauté 5 min. or until onions are translucent. Add wine; cook over high heat until liquid is reduced by half.

Wrap thyme, bay leaves and peppercorns in cheesecloth; tie closed. Add to ingredients in pan along with all remaining ingredients except salt, black pepper and parsley; mix well.

Return lamb to pan; cover. Simmer over medium-low heat 3 hours, or until entirely tender. (At this point, you can take the shanks off the heat and, after they have cooled, refrigerate them overnight or until needed. Just before serving, remove the layer of fat off the surface and discard, then reheat the shanks in the sauce.)

Remove and discard wrapped herbs. If necessary, remove the meat and keep warm while you cook the sauce a bit more to thicken. Season with salt and black pepper. Plate the shanks and top with sauce. Garnish with chopped parsley.

VENISON CHILI WITH BLACK BEANS AND HONEY-SPICED ONION CRISPS

GLORIA CICCARONE-NEHLS of the Huntington Hotel in San Francisco was kind enough to share her venison chili recipe with me. The heat comes from both jalapeños and chili sauce, and the beans are not stewed with the meat but added as a garnish. The chili in its own right is a great dish, with aniseed and ground cloves among the many seasonings, but the topping of honey-spiced onion crisps takes it to another level. You can substitute beef chuck for the venison.

Makes 10 servings

Chili

2 fresh jalapeño peppers
¼ cup olive oil
6 cloves garlic
¼ cup vegetable oil
3 lb. ground venison or ground beef
2 lb. ground pork
3 yellow onions, sliced
3 Tbsp. chili powder
2 Tbsp. ground cumin
1 Tbsp. dried thyme leaves
2 tsp. salt
1 tsp. each black pepper, celery seed,
*   dried oregano leaves and paprika*
½ tsp. each aniseed, cayenne pepper
*   and crushed red pepper*
Dash of ground cloves
3 bottles (10 oz. each) chili sauce
2 cans (28 oz. each) diced tomatoes,
*   lightly drained*
3 cups chicken stock or broth
*   (purchased or homemade)*
1 cup tomato paste
2 bay leaves

Recipe continues on page 148

Recipe continued from page 146

Honey-Spiced Onion Crisps
2 qt. (8 cups) canola oil, for frying
2 ½ tsp. each chili powder, ground cumin and salt
½ tsp. cayenne pepper
3 very firm red onions, 250 g each,
  thinly sliced, separated into rings
2 Tbsp. honey
About 2 cups flour (for dusting)

Additional Chili Toppings
2 cups drained cooked black beans
2 cups shredded sharp white Cheddar cheese

Chili
Stem and seed jalapeños and remove membranes. Coarsely chop and transfer to blender. Add olive oil and garlic. Process in blender until puréed; set aside.

Heat vegetable oil in 12-qt. stockpot over medium heat. Add meat; cook until evenly browned, stirring occasionally. Add jalapeño purée, onions and dry seasonings; stir. Cook 5 min. Add remaining ingredients; mix well. Bring to boil. Reduce heat; simmer 2 to 2½ hours, stirring frequently. Meanwhile, prepare onion crisps.

Honey-Spiced Onion Crisps
Heat canola oil in deep fryer to 375°F. Meanwhile, place onions in a large bowl and toss with combined dry seasonings. Transfer to a second large bowl and then toss with honey to coat. Sift flour and into a third large bowl. Working in small batches, add onions to the flour and toss with fork to coat. Transfer to a sieve and shake off excess flour. Continue with ¼-cup batches of remaining flour until onions are evenly coated but not caked with flour, sifting every time. Let stand a few minutes. Transfer to a sieve and shake well. Toss again to remove excess flour.

Layer paper towels on work surface to drain fried onions on. Fry onions, in hot oil until crisp and golden brown but not burned, using skimmer to transfer cooked onions from each batch to paper towels.

Repeat with remaining onions, sifting flour before adding each batch to the bowl and taking care to shake off the excess.

Serving Directions
Heat beans. Bring chili back to a simmer if necessary; remove and discard bay leaves. Spoon chili into serving bowls. Top with beans, cheese and onion crisps.

VEGETABLES

CAULIFLOWER WITH CURRY BUTTER

THIS IS A COMPOSITE of several recipes that I put together one year when I needed a cauliflower side dish for Thanksgiving. A bonus on the busiest day for cooking: You can make this well in advance, then reheat it just before serving.

Makes 4 to 6 servings

3 lb. cauliflower florets,
  weighed after stems removed
½ cup golden raisins
5 Tbsp. butter, melted
1 Tbsp. lemon juice
1 tsp. curry powder
¼ tsp. ground cumin
⅛ tsp. cayenne
Salt and pepper, to taste
Chopped fresh chives (for garnish)

Heat oven to 400°F.

Bring large pot of salted water to boil. Meanwhile, cut cauliflower into small florets.

Add cauliflower, in batches, to boiling water; cook 1 to 2 min. or just until cauliflower is tender. (Do not overcook – cauliflower should still be firm.) Use slotted spoon to transfer cauliflower to colander; drain well. Place in large bowl.

Combine all remaining ingredients except chives. Add to cauliflower; mix lightly, being careful to not break florets. Spoon into ovenproof serving dish.

Bake 10 min. or until thoroughly heated. Garnish with chives.

TIP
• Before cooking, the cauliflower can be kept at room temperature for 2 to 3 hours, or covered and refrigerated and then brought to room temperature. Cauliflower also can be cooked, then tossed with remaining ingredients ahead of time. Cool, then let stand at room temperature up to 3 hours. To reheat, bake in 400°F oven 10 minutes, or until heated through. Garnish with chives. Or cover and refrigerate up to 24 hours. Bring to room temperature, then reheat.

MASHED POTATOES

THE TRICK of cooking potatoes in milk was given to me by Pierre Mondard of Lenôtre in Paris, and it really does make a difference. Be sure to drain the potatoes very, very well after they finish cooking; otherwise they get watery. To make them taste even more luxurious, substitute truffle butter for the regular butter and season with truffle salt.

Makes 4 to 6 servings

2 to 2½ lbs. Yukon gold potatoes
3 to 4 cups milk
⅓ cup heavy cream
3 to 4 Tbsp. butter, at room temperature
½ cup finely chopped fresh chives (optional)
1 tsp. kosher salt, or to taste
½ tsp. white pepper, or to taste

Peel potatoes; cut into thirds. (Or, if potatoes are large, quarter them lengthwise instead.) Place in large saucepan. Add equal amounts of milk and water until potatoes are completely covered. Bring to boil; simmer until potatoes are tender. (Potatoes should almost be falling apart.) Drain well in a colander or strainer, discarding liquid.

Heat cream and butter in top of double boiler. Use ricer to rice the potatoes; press potatoes to remove small amount of liquid, then add potatoes to warm cream mixture. Be careful not to overchurn or the potatoes will not be fluffy. Stir in chives, salt and pepper and serve.

TIP

• *Potatoes can be cooked ahead of time. Prepare recipe as directed, except do not stir in the chives. Cool, cover, then let stand at room temperature up to 2 hours before reheating just before serving, stirring in enough additional cream until the desired consistency is reached. Stir in chives.*

GLAZED CARROTS

HERE IS AN EASY WAY to add layers of flavor to a vegetable that too often is served with nothing more exciting than butter. Cumin and cilantro greatly enhance the taste.

Makes 4 servings

10 large carrots, peeled, cut into 2-inch chunks
1 cup fresh cilantro,
    stems removed, coarsely chopped
¼ cup butter
3 Tbsp. sugar
2 tsp. ground cumin
1 qt. (4 cups) chicken stock or broth
    (purchased or homemade)
Salt and pepper, to taste
15 to 20 fresh whole cilantro leaves,
    chiffonade (for garnish)

Place carrots, chopped cilantro, butter, sugar and cumin in large saucepan. Add enough chicken stock to cover all ingredients. Bring to boil; simmer until carrots are almost done. Use slotted spoon to transfer carrots to bowl; set aside. Return broth mixture to boil; simmer until reduced to almost to a glaze-like consistency (about ½ cup). Return carrots to saucepan; stir to evenly coat with glaze. Season with salt and pepper. Use tongs to transfer carrots to serving plate. Garnish with cilantro.

TIP
• *Carrots and glaze can be cooked ahead of time. Cool, then refrigerate (separately) several days before serving. Reheat glaze, then stir in carrots and cook until heated through.*

ROASTED CIPOLLINE ONIONS

I PREFER ONIONS cooked in duck fat, but coconut oil works well. The balsamic vinegar is a great addition. Parboiling the onions also makes them easier to peel. For best results, use onions of similar size. The recipe was given to me by Ricky Soares, the chef who works with my brother and sister-in-law on Long Island.

Makes 4 to 6 servings

1 lb. (about 60 to 70) cipolline onions (unpeeled)
2 tsp. salt
½ tsp. freshly ground black pepper, or to taste
⅓ cup good-quality balsamic vinegar
¼ cup coconut oil
¼ cup beef stock or veal stock
¼ cup white wine

Bring large pot of salted water to a rolling oil. Add onions and cook 1 minute. Remove from water and let cool.

Using a small sharp knife, trim top and bottom off each onion and remove about 2 layers of peel. Return to boiling salted water and cook 5 to 7 minutes, or until they start to soften.

When onions are done, drain and coat with vinegar and oil while still warm. Spread in roasting pan and cook at 375 degrees for 15 to 20 minutes, or until soft but still with more cooking needed. Remove from oven and add stock and wine to pan to coat onions. Continue cooking until onions are softened and caramelized, 20 to 30 minutes. Set aside.

Just before serving, remove onions from marinade and reheat at 400 degrees for 10 to 15 minutes, until slightly crispy. Be careful not to burn.

ROASTED FINGERLING POTATOS

I PREFER FINGERLINGS to any other potatoes. This recipe, using duck fat, should give you potatoes that are crispy on the outside and soft on the inside. Start with potatoes of similar size so that they cook evenly.

Makes 5 servings

2 Tbsp. duck fat or olive oil
20 fingerling potatoes (about 2 lbs.), cut in half
1 Tbsp. kosher salt, or more to taste
2 tsp. freshly ground black pepper
3 Tbsp. aged good-quality balsamic vinegar

Heat oven to 400°F.

Heat duck fat or olive oil in a large iron skillet. Season potatoes with salt and pepper and arrange in pan, cut sides down. Cook until they start to brown, about 12 minutes, then turn them over. Transfer to the oven and bake until they are hard outside and soft inside, 5 to 10 minutes longer. Toss with balsamic vinegar and adjust salt and pepper if needed.

TWO-CHEESE CREAMED SPINACH

THIS RECIPE IS INSPIRED by several versions of the classic side dish I have tried in many steakhouses. The combination of two cheeses and triple truffle flavorings takes it to a higher level. Using pre-washed baby spinach lets you skip both the rinsing and the stemming tedium of the prep work.

Makes 4 servings

2 pounds baby spinach
4 to 6 Tbsp butter, preferably truffle butter
5 Tbsp minced white onion
4 to 6 Tbsp heavy cream
¾ cup grated Comte Gruyere
¾ cup grated Parmigiano Reggiano
2 to 3 Tbsp white truffle oil
Salt and freshly ground black pepper to taste
  (use truffle salt if possible)

Cook spinach in a large pan over low heat, adding leaves about 2 cups at a time, until just wilted. Remove from heat and cool. Squeeze spinach dry, then chop roughly. (You can make the recipe ahead to this point, just refrigerate until needed.)

Melt the butter in the pan and sauté the onion until softened, then add the spinach and cream to the pan. Stir in both cheeses and cook just until incorporated. Add the truffle oil to taste and season with salt and pepper to taste.

ROASTED PLUM TOMATOES

SLOW-COOKING plum tomatoes makes for a wonderful vegetable or accompaniment. These are best in the middle of the summer into the fall, when tomatoes are ripest and sweetest, although this technique can make even winter tomatoes taste summery. They are good on their own or topped with fresh mozzarella or pesto, or with both. They also make a tasty and colorful garnish.

Makes 3 to 4 servings

10 plum tomatoes
Olive oil
Salt and pepper, to taste

Heat oven to 250°F.

Cut tomatoes in half; use fingers to gently remove seeds and juice.

Place in roasting pan; drizzle lightly with oil. Sprinkle with salt and pepper.

Bake 2 to 4 hours or until tomatoes are wilted and deep red in color, depending on how you like them. Serve hot or cooled.

SAVORY MASHED YAMS

THIS RECIPE GIVES you the benefit of a white potato consistency with sweetness and more flavor. When you mix in the maple syrup and nutmeg, these yams are spectacular.

Makes 6 to 8 servings

6 medium yams (4 lbs./2724 g)
2 Tbsp. olive oil
5 Tbsp. butter
2 Tbsp. maple syrup
1 tsp. grated nutmeg
Salt and pepper, to taste

Heat oven to 400°F.

Rub yams with oil; place on foil-covered baking sheet.

Bake 40 to 50 min. or until thoroughly cooked. (Tip of sharp knife should easily pierce centers of yams.) Cool slightly.

Peel yams; place yam flesh in medium bowl. Mash using potato ricer or masher until desired consistency. Add remaining ingredients; mix well. Serve immediately. (These can be reheated.)

TRUFFLED HARICOTS VERTS

THIS IS A VARIATION on my spinach recipe but even simpler. You can substitute regular green beans when they are in season locally because those are so great.

Makes 4 to 5 servings

1¼ pounds haricots verts, tips removed
4 ounces truffle butter
¼ cup truffle oil
Truffle salt to taste
Freshly ground black pepper

Steam the beans until al dente, about 5 minutes. Immediately blanch in cold water. Just before serving, reheat with truffle butter, truffle oil and salt along with some freshly ground black pepper.

PUREE OF PEAS WITH MINT, CILANTRO & SCALLIONS

THIS IS AN INTERESTING approach to peas — puréeing them releases their sweetness, and the intensity of the herbs is unusual.

Makes 4 servings

1 lb. (454 g) frozen peas
½ cup fresh cilantro
½ cup fresh mint
1 Tbsp. butter
1 Tbsp. olive oil
2 tsp. chopped fresh jalapeño peppers
1 tsp. sugar
1 Tbsp. finely chopped scallions (white parts only)
½ tsp. salt
Black pepper and additional salt, to taste

Bring 3 to 4 cups salted water to boil in large saucepan. Add peas; return to boil. Cook 2 min.; drain, reserving 2 Tbsp. of the cooking water.

Transfer peas to food processor. Add reserved cooking water and all remaining ingredients except black pepper and additional salt; process until smooth. Stir in scallions. Season with pepper and additional salt.

TIP
• *For more or less heat, adjust the measure of jalapeño peppers used.*

ROASTED BRUSSELS SPROUTS

STARTING THE Brussels sprouts in a cast-iron skillet on top of the stove and finishing them in a hot oven gives good caramelization. The trick with Brussels sprouts is the same as for baby artichokes: You have to be aggressive in peeling off the outer leaves, at least two to three layers' worth, to get to the tender parts. Balsamic vinegar and piment d' Espelette elevate the flavor.

Makes 4 servings

1 lb. medium-large Brussels sprouts
1 Tbsp. butter, softened
Piment d'Espelette, to taste
Salt and pepper, to taste
5 Tbsp. olive oil
2 Tbsp. maple syrup
1 Tbsp. balsamic vinegar

Heat oven to 400°F.

Trim bottoms off Brussels sprouts; cut sprouts lengthwise in half. Remove and discard any tough outer leaves; place trimmed sprouts in large bowl.

Mix butter, piment d'Espelette, salt and pepper until blended. Add to Brussels sprouts; toss until evenly coated.

Heat oil in large iron skillet until oil starts to shimmer. Add Brussels sprouts, cut sides down; cook until lightly browned.

Place skillet in oven. Bake 15 min. or until sprouts are roasted to desired doneness, turning occasionally and reducing the heat if necessary to prevent sprouts from burning.

Return sprouts to bowl. Add syrup and vinegar; toss until sprouts are evenly coated. Season with additional salt, pepper and piment d'Espelette, if desired.

DESSERTS

CHOCOLATE TERRINE WITH CRÈME ANGLAISE

BACK IN THE EARLY Eighties I purchased the Grand-Hotel du Cap-Ferrat for a company I was president of called Reliance Development, a subsidiary of Reliance Group Holdings, and we ran and subsequently renovated the hotel. The chef at the time was Jean-Claude Guillon, and he was kind enough to give me cooking lessons during the approximately five years we owned the hotel. He taught me this chocolate terrine, which was really quite special, and I continue to serve it.

Makes 6 to 8 servings

Chocolate Terrine
7 oz. (200 g) butter (room temperature)
10½ oz. (300 g) bittersweet chocolate, melted
2 Tbsp. water
8 eggs, separated, divided use
3 Tbsp. sugar, divided use

Crème Anglaise
500 ML whole milk
500 ML heavy cream
1 vanilla bean, split in half
8 egg yolks
200 g sugar

Chocolate Terrine
Whisk butter, chocolate and water in medium bowl until blended.

Cook egg yolks and 1 Tbsp. sugar in top of double boiler until thickened, stirring occasionally. Gradually stir into chocolate mixture. Place in ice water bath; let stand until chilled, stirring occasionally.

Beat egg whites and remaining 2 Tbsp. sugar with mixer on high speed until stiff peaks form. Fold into chocolate mixture.

Refrigerate 6 hours or until chilled.

Crème Anglaise
Mix milk and cream in medium saucepan. Scrape seeds from vanilla bean halves into saucepan. Add scraped beans; stir. Bring just to simmer. Remove from heat.

Beat egg yolks and sugar in medium bowl with whisk until blended. Gradually add hot milk mixture, whisking well after each addition. Return milk mixture to saucepan.

Cook over low heat 5 min. or until thickened. Pour through strainer into bowl. Refrigerate until chilled and ready to serve.

Slice terrine and serve with Crème Anglaise.

TIPS
• *This versatile dessert sauce can be refrigerated up to 24 hours before using as desired.*

• *For best results, use any 70% or over 70% cacao chocolate.*

MOUSSE AU CHOCOLAT

THIS IS SIMPLE and quick and always a big hit. You can make it up to five days in advance and store it in the refrigerator. I think I picked this recipe up in 1970 out of the New York Times. (Anything that's that old you can steal.)

Makes 6 servings

½ lb. (227 g) semisweet chocolate
  (56 to 62% cacao), coarsely chopped
¾ cup (6 oz.) butter, cut into small pieces
6 large eggs, separated
Dash of salt
½ cup superfine sugar

Place chocolate in medium saucepan over large saucepan partially filled with simmering water. (Water should not be boiling or touch bottom of smaller chocolate-filled saucepan.) Cook over low heat until chocolate is completely melted. Add butter; stir until melted. Remove from heat; cool slightly.

Beat egg whites and salt in a bowl with mixer on high speed until stiff peaks form. Set aside.

Beat egg yolks and sugar in large bowl with mixer on high speed 4 min. or until thick and lemon colored. Add to chocolate mixture; stir with whisk just until blended. Fold in egg whites. Pour into serving bowl.

Refrigerate several hours or until chilled.

TIP
• *If you don't have super-fine sugar, put a little more than half a cup of sugar in the Cuisinart or a food processor to produce the amount needed here.*

FRUIT SALAD

THIS FRUIT SALAD was taught to me by Pierre Mondard of Lenôtre in Paris. It's better than other fruit salads because the combination of lemon juice with the crunchiness of the apple and the chiffonade of mint puts it over the top. You can make it with any fruit as long as you use apples, as well as the lemon juice and chiffonade of mint.

Makes 4 to 6 servings

1/4 ~~1¼~~ *cup water*
¼ cup sugar
2 Tbsp. lemon juice
5 cups cut-up mixed seasonal fresh fruit,
    such as berries, melon, oranges and/or peaches
1 cup peeled, cored and chopped apples
⅓ cup fresh mint in chiffonade

Bring water and sugar to boil in saucepan; cook until sugar is dissolved, stirring occasionally. Stir in juice; cool. Refrigerate until chilled.

Meanwhile, combine fruit. Refrigerate until ready to serve.

Add the lemon syrup and mint to fruit just before serving; mix lightly.

CHOCOLATE CAKE

THIS RECIPE ADAPTED from the River Cafe in London is best known for being troublesome. However, I figured out how to make it work: Half the time it has to cook more. You can't rely on timing. You have to bake it until it's absolutely firm to the touch. It could take an hour, it could take an hour and a half.

Makes 8 to 10 servings

2 sticks plus 1 Tbsp. unsalted butter, divided use
12 oz. semisweet chocolate (70% cacao)
1 cup superfine sugar, divided use
7 Tbsp. Water
5 eggs

Heat oven to 300°F.

Grease sides and bottom of 10-inch round cake pan with ½ Tbsp. of the butter. Line with parchment paper; brush with ½ Tbsp. of the remaining butter. Dust pans lightly with flour.

Break chocolate into small pieces; place in bowl with remaining butter over pan of simmering (not boiling) water. Heat until melted. Meanwhile, cook ¾ cup sugar and 7 Tbsp. water in separate pan until sugar is completely dissolved.

Add hot sugar syrup to melted chocolate; mix well. Cool slightly.

Beat eggs and remaining ¼ cup sugar in small bowl with mixer on high speed until quadrupled in volume. Add chocolate mixture; beat on low speed just until blended. Pour into prepared pan.

Place folded dish towel in roasting pan; top with filled cake pan. Add enough hot water to roasting pan to come ¾ of the way up side of cake pan.

Bake 1 hour to 1 hour and a half, or until the center of the cake is firm to the touch. Let cake stand in water in roasting pan 30 min. or until cooled. Run knife around edge of pan to loosen cake. Invert pan onto serving plate; let stand until cake releases from pan onto plate. Remove pan.

TIPS
• *If the cake sticks to the bottom of the pan, place the bottom of the pan in very hot water. Let stand a few minutes. Remove from water. Let stand 15 to 20 min., then try to unmold again. (If the cake is still recalcitrant, whack the bottom of the pan with a heavy pot or skillet.)*

• *Since this is a rich cake, be sure to serve it in small portions.*

TARTE TATIN

I DON'T KNOW where I acquired this recipe, but it is the best tarte Tatin. The whole trick is to pay attention to the moment when pan-cooking the apples that the sugar and butter take on a deep brown color, just before they get black. When you unmold the tarte, carefully take any bits of apples that might have stuck to the pan and fit them back onto the dessert. If you don't have a proper tarte Tatin mold, use a heavy 10-inch nonstick, ovenproof skillet instead.

Recipe continues on page 170

Recipe continued from page 169

Makes 6 servings

Flour (for dusting)
1 pkg. (14 oz.) Dufour frozen puff pastry
  (1 sheet), thawed
6 medium Golden Delicious or Gala apples,
  peeled, cored and each cut into 8 wedges
1 Tbsp. ground cinnamon
3 Tbsp. unsalted butter, at room temperature
⅔ cup sugar
1 egg, lightly beaten with a little water

Roll out pastry on lightly floured surface to circle ½ inch larger than top of 10-inch tarte Tatin mold. Fold up edge of dough to make ½-inch-high rim. Refrigerate until ready to use.

Toss apple wedges with cinnamon in large bowl; set aside.

Spread butter onto bottom and up side of Tatin mold; sprinkle with sugar. Gently shake mold to evenly coat bottom with sugar.

Arrange single layer of apple wedges, rounded sides down, in concentric circles on bottom of mold, starting at outer edge and working toward center, placing apples as closey together as possible. Insert any remaining apple slices into spaces between apple slices in mold.

Cook over low heat just until butter is melted. Increase heat to medium-high. Cook (without stirring) 30 min. or until sugar turns deep golden brown. (Be careful to not let burn.) Remove from heat. Use back of wooden spoon to gently press down apples to help fill any spaces between them.

Heat oven to 350°F. Brush rim of pastry with egg wash; place, rim side down, over apples in mold; carefully tuck edge of pastry between apples and inside edge of mold to seal.

Bake 30 min. or until pastry is a deep golden mahogany brown color. Cool 20 min.

Place serving plate over mold, then flip mold and plate together to unmold. Remove mold. Let stand 20 min. If any apples have stuck to bottom of mold, use two forks to gently remove apples and then reposition them on tart. Cool completely before serving.

TIPS
• *When baking the tatin, rotate the mold in the oven, if necessary, for even browning.*

• *Use an 8-section apple corer/cutter to quickly cut the apples into wedges.*

LEMON TART

DANNY BROWN, the chef at X Bar on the Upper East Side of Manhattan, was kind enough to share this easy dinner party dessert. The recipe for the dough makes enough for two crusts, which I prefer because it gives you a head start on a future tart. You can keep the second one, tightly sealed, for up to a week in the refrigerator or for months in the freezer.

Makes 8 servings

Pate Sucrée
3⅓ cups flour, plus extra for rolling
7 oz. cold butter, cubed, plus extra for tart pans
1 cup sugar
3 egg yolks
1 tsp. salt
1 tbsp. cold water (optional)

Lemon Curd
2 large eggs
2 large egg yolks
¾ cup sugar
½ cup fresh lemon juice
6 Tbsp. cold unsalted butter, cut into 6 pieces

Pate Sucrée
Sift the flour into the bowl of a KitchenAid mixer. With the motor running on low, gently add the butter bit by bit until well incorporated. Add the sugar, egg yolks and salt and mix until smooth. You may need to add the water to bring the dough together. Turn out onto a floured surface and knead once or twice. Divide into 2 parts. Shape each into a disk and cover in plastic wrap. Transfer the dough to the refrigerator and let rest at least 1 hour but preferably overnight.

Butter and flour a 9 inch tart pan. Roll one disk of dough out on a lightly floured surface and carefully lay into the prepared pan. Trim off the excess. Place in the refrigerator and chill until firm. Store the second disk of dough in the refrigerator or freezer until needed.

Heat the oven to 350 degrees. Cut a sheet of baking parchment to fit into the tart pan. Line with pie weights. Bake the crust 20 minutes. Remove the weights and parchment and return the crust to the oven to bake 10 minutes longer. Remove from the oven and dock the crust with a fork. Using a pastry brush, gently brush the tart shell with water and set aside to cool completely.

Lemon Curd
In a bowl whisk the eggs, egg yolks and sugar until smooth.

Set the bowl over a pot filled with boiling water. Whip the egg mixture while turning the bowl. When the mixture is foamy and has thickened, add a third of the lemon juice.

Continue to whisk. When mixture thickens again, add a third more of the lemon juice. Repeat with remaining lemon juice. Turn off the heat but leave the bowl over the pot. Add the cold butter piece by piece until well-incorporated. Let cool completely before spooning into the prepared crust.

GRILLED FIGS WITH AMARETTO

MY FRIEND David Detone was kind enough to share this easy summer dessert with me. You could also try it with ripe peaches, apricots or nectarines.

Makes 4 servings

10 to 12 amaretti
¼ cup honey
¼ cup Amaretto (or enough to soak the figs)
Small amount of oil for grill or griddle
Any amount of figs, halved lengthwise
Yogurt or ice cream for garnish
Mint leaves in chiffonade for garnish

Break up the amaretti in the Cuisinart to make crumbs. Set aside.

Combine the honey and Amaretto in a bowl large enough to hold the halved figs. Set aside.

Heat the grill or griddle. Lightly oil it. Lay the figs on, cut side down, and cook briefly.

Transfer the figs to the bowl and gently toss with the Amaretto-honey mixture. Top each fig with a teaspoon or so of the amaretti crumbs. Garnish with yogurt or ice cream and top with mint chiffonade.

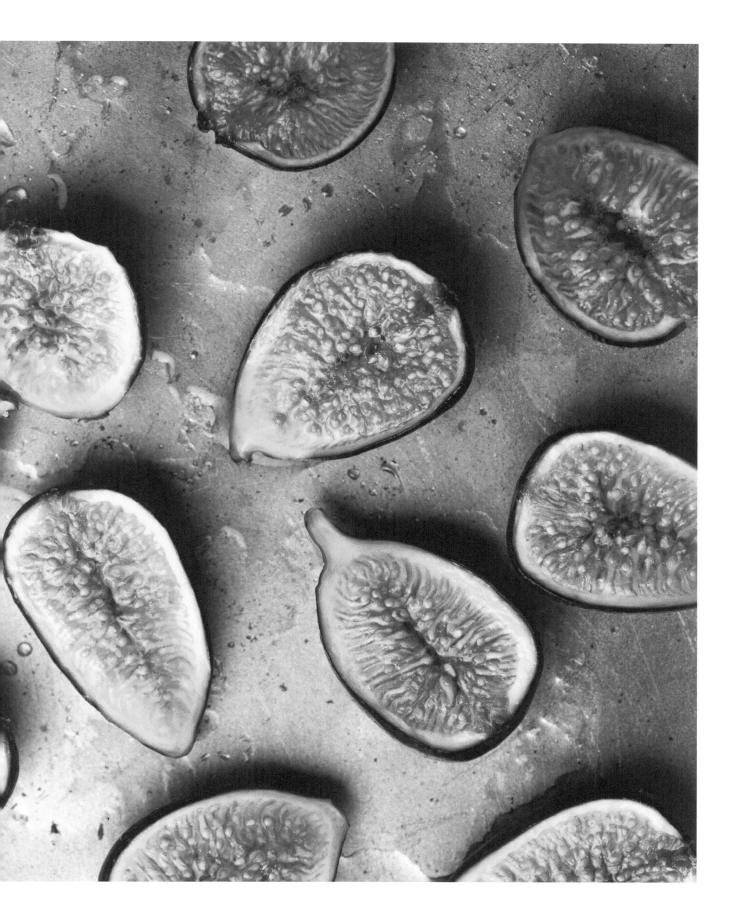

HELLO DOLLIES

MY FRIEND Tracey Goetz in North Carolina gave me the best Christmas cookie recipe.

Makes 24 bars

1 stick butter
1 cup crushed graham cracker crumbs
12 ounces semisweet chocolate chips
1½ cups chopped walnuts
12-ounce can Borden's Eagle Brand
  condensed milk

Heat oven to 350 degrees.

Melt butter in oven in 9- by 13-inch baking dish. Sprinkle graham cracker crumbs over the bottom of the pan. Spread chocolate chips over that, then the walnuts. Pour the condensed milk over and bake 30 minutes, or until golden brown. Cool before cutting into squares.

BLUEBERRY COMPOTE

THIS EASY (if expensive in wintertime) dessert comes from my collaborator Douglas Parreira. Serve it warm over vanilla ice cream, or with cheesecake.

Makes 6 servings

5 half-pint containers blueberries,
  as sweet as you can get
½ cup water
¼ cup sugar
¼ cup lemon juice

Combine 4 of the containers of blueberries in a saucepan over a low flame. Cook about 1 hour. Add the remaining berries and cook about an hour longer. If the berries get too sticky, add a little more water. If you make this in advance, reheat just before serving.

Night Cafe
Etching in brown/black ink • Edvard Munch, Norway 1901
Bequest of Scofield Thayer, 1982

A Kitchen Scene
Engraving • After David Vinckboons (Netherlandish, Mechelen 1576–1629 Amsterdam)
The Elisha Whittelsey Collection, 1957

THE METROPOLITAN MUSEUM OF ART • NEW YORK NY

THE ESSENTIAL LAMBERT PANTRY

Lesieur mayonnaise I grew up like most people, thinking Hellmann's (or Best Foods) mayonnaise was the best thing since sliced bread. Then I discovered Lesieur in France, and it is so much better. I used to make my own mayonnaise, but since I found this it's just not worth the effort. If you can't fly to France, or St. Barts, and bring jars of this back in your suitcase, you can buy it on Amazon. Be sure to get the regular version, not the one made without mustard.

Thai sweet chile sauce I was at a restaurant in St. Barts called Tamarind and asked what made the tuna tartare so good. They told me it was this sauce, and I've been using it ever since. It's a terrific flavor enhancer.

Honeycup mustard This sweet but sharp mustard is essential in my smoked salmon appetizer. But it also makes all the difference on any meats, too. On smoked turkey it's spectacular.

Lambrusco vinegar Steven Jenkins, whom I worked with at Pasta & Cheese and who went on to become a star at Fairway markets, put me on to this outstanding vinegar. It's made from the grapes usually used in a slightly fizzy and wonderful Italian wine. Everyone I know who has tried it never goes back to regular red wine vinegar.

Balsamic vinegar I never realized balsamic vinegar was that much better until I found the Elsa brand. Then my friend Nancy McNally gave me a bottle of Ritrova Selections balsamic. I find that either of these is good enough that I end up enjoying them on their own.

Smoked salmon I have tried all types of smoked salmon, from Norwegian to Nova Scotian, but Irish is the one I return to every time. It's not easy to find, but Agata & Valentina in New York City carries it.

Minor's crab and lobster bases I used to spend forever collecting crab and lobster shells and making broth from them, and then I discovered these excellent concentrates, thanks to a restaurant in Jacksonville, Florida. The manufacturer uses the same process I would but on a mass scale. These really do the trick in soups and sauces.

Piment d'Espelette Jean Claude Dufour, the chef at Restaurant L'Esprit in St. Barts, uses this Basque chile pepper to season his tuna, and I discovered it's a wonderful addition to other dishes that are sautéed or broiled. It gives a whole new dimension and more complexity than regular pepper.

Tutto Calabria Hot Red Pepper Jelly If you make a ham and cheese sandwich with this, it lifts everything. It's spicy and sweet and just lifts all the other flavors. As with anything these days, you can find it on Amazon.

Sriracha I substitute this for almost any hot sauce now. I think horseradish is done . . .

COOK'S TIPS

A BACON BIT

If you want perfect bacon, for the lentil salad or other recipes, here is the best technique: Buy slab bacon, slice it thick and bake it on a sheet of parchment at 375 degrees, turning once until it's as crisp as you like it. Chris Gorney, the assistant manager and chef at the Southampton Bath and Tennis Club, was kind enough to teach me this technique.

HOW TO BOIL AN EGG

Steam it. Start with a large egg (60 to 65 grams). Put it in a steamer basket in a pot filled with slowly boiling water for 13 minutes (7 minutes for a quail egg). Transfer to ice-cold water and let it sit for 10 to 15 minutes and the shell will peel right off.

PRO(DUCE) TIPS

•When a recipe calls for onions, know that Spanish onions are sweeter. Or: When in doubt, always use Spanish.

• If you live in my part of the country, it's a waste of money to buy melons anytime but late summer when they are in season. The only fruits worthwhile to buy out of season are pineapples and berries if you like sweetness. But if you do buy pineapple, invest two to three days in advance. Stores never have any ripe ones because those are all cut up for containers, so they can get higher prices. You have to warehouse fruit yourself.

•You really want to get artichokes and asparagus in season, when they are gorgeous and big. Just a month on, you should be buying green beans \/haricots vert.

•To cook artichokes just right, start by choosing green ones that do not look dried out. Using a chef's knife, cut off each stem as well as 1½ inches off the top of each. Using scissors, trim the prickly ends off the leaves. Slice a lemon ¼ inch thick and, using kitchen twine, tie a slice to the bottom of each artichoke, Steam, bottoms down, until done, 20 to 40 minutes, testing after 20 minutes — a fork should slide into the bottoms easily. Take out and drain upside-down until easy to handle. Using a spoon, scoop out the hard center, then scrape the remaining choke from the heart. Serve warm or cold, with vinaigrette.

LITERAL KNIFE TIPS

Like most cooks, I am often asked which knives I consider most indispensable. My arsenal holds five: a chef's knife, a large Asian knife, a paring knife, a boning knife and a serrated knife. Those will get any job done. A utility knife, one with a blade you don't mind wrecking, is also useful for things like opening plastic packaging.

My Santoku seven-inch knife is the one I use for most things because it does everything: chop, slice, dice — everything. It's also best for detail work, like chopping chives.

My boning knife is also good not just for separating meat from flesh but for removing the rind from a melon.

My serrated knife is good for slicing bread (and also tomatoes).

For small jobs I use my paring knife.

And I only use my large chef's knife for things like taking the tops off artichokes, when I need something with power.

A FEW MEAT TIPS

For some advice on buying beef, I spent time with Ray Venezia, a well-known butcher at Fairway Markets who has written a book on the subject. He says it's most important to choose prime beef that has been aged in a way that keeps moisture loss to a minimum. Aging is a process of decomposition done in a positive way: It tenderizes the meat and adds flavor as the fibers break down. Butcher-aged beef is done in a controlled environment, while supermarkets package the meat so that it is not aging but just leaching juices in its plastic packaging.

My own advice is on steak: When you buy a piece of that prime beef for two people, buy one piece in double thickness and then slice it after grilling. Don't buy two 1-inch-thick steaks but one that is 1½ to 1¾ inches thick. Good,

tasty meat is meat with moisture, and a thicker steak on the grill will cook through without drying out. Then you let it sit long enough for the juices to redistribute. Don't carve it until you can hold it in your hand.

With poultry, if you have a choice always buy less heavy birds, whether chicken or turkey. They're more tender because they're younger.

SECRETS OF CHEESE STORAGE

James Coogan, cheesemonger for Eli Zabar in NYC, has this advice to offer:

Always serve cheese at room temperature. If you're planning an afternoon party, remove cheeses from the refrigerator six to eight hours in advance. Much like with a glass of white wine served too cold, the flavors of cheese can't be tasted when masked by low temperatures.

Most cheeses are less perishable than credited; cheese is controlled spoilage, after all. If a bit of mold grows on the outside, scrape it off. No big deal. Unless a cheese looks like a total science experiment, don't throw it out! While plastic wrap is necessary in retail, other methods are more optimal for extended storage. Products specifically designed for storage (e.g Formaticum cheese paper and storage bags) or wax paper work better. Store cheese in the least cold part of the fridge — a vegetable crisper works well, but farthest from the freezer is ideal in a conventional refrigerator.

OLIVE OIL WISDOM FROM A MASTER, STEVEN JENKINS

If you follow these rules of mine wherever you choose to select and replenish your olive oil, you will not have lousy olive oil in your life.

1. Read the fine print on the label; make sure the olive oil in that container has a label that freely states the year the olives were milled, the oil created. If it's late last year, it's fine. If it's two years old already, you're in one of those supermarkets that is clueless about olive oil. This is often the case in the nicest specialty food shops, too, so beware.

2. The oil must be either in a tin or a dark bottle. Clear bottles are anathema to olive oil, and no self-respecting miller would allow his olive oil to wind up in a clear bottle. The color green is but chlorophyll, and has no bearing on quality, though it often does suggest an early harvest oil. Light is merciless in leaching out the green, reducing olive oil to a limpid yellow rather than a healthy, striking gold. Light also leaches out the very vitamins within olive oil, yep, right through the glass. Heat, oxygen and time are the other enemies. Olive oil does not improve with age.

3. Demand that the label tell you where the olives and oil came from. This will be a town or city close to the groves. Now your job is to determine in which region of which country that town or city lies. Country has no bearing whatsoever on the quality of olive oil. Don't let anyone make you believe "the best olive oil comes from _____." That person doesn't know what he or she is talking about. A grasp of Mediterranean Basin geography is crucial to understanding olive oil. Get out your maps; go on-line for a map. If you don't know where Partanna is in Sicily, you don't deserve to have great olive oil. If you don't know where Sicily is, or Corsica, or Crete, or Catalonia, or Sardinia, I give up.

4. Strive to select only olive oils whose labels state boldly that the oil is EARLY HARVEST. This is crucial, because it is the underripe green olives that offer the highest phenol counts, the free radicals, that not only are the healthiest thing in the world (anti-aging, anti-oxidizing, etc., etc.) but are the very meaning of the finest of olive oils, that is, those that are pungent, peppery and a bit bitter; that make you cough, that make you understand that the finest olive oil is not a food to be tasted in the manner of wine, but is a condiment. It is that bitterness — that very bitterness — that serves to amplify the flavors of all it touches — anoints, bastes, marinates, dresses. I'm not suggesting that you cook with this most expensive of olive oils, but I do -- as do all of us who revere olive oil. You are permitted to

keep around a liter or two of a less expensive though still noble olive oil. Just not one you bought for five or six bucks a liter. I would, in a trusted supermarket, allow you to spend ten or twelve, but only for frying.

The best olive oils in the world will cost around $30 to $40 per liter; $15 to $20 per half-liter; $22.50 to $30 per 750ml containers (many, many 750ml containers out there). Pay attention to the size of the container.

Late harvest olives result in a lot more yield for the grower/miller. These olive oils are often termed "fruity", a dead giveaway for stupid olive oil that will lie on your food like a side of lox and will not be your long-life-ensuring, free-of-disease friend.

I could go on, but these four edicts should suffice. I trust that the more you use and taste your early harvest monocultivars (single variety), the more your eyes will light up when you taste fresh, warm mozzarella drizzled with them, the more you exult over the vinaigrette you create for your glorious salads, the more you find true joy when they are dribbled over hot bread and pizza, the more perspicacious about this most crucial ingredient you will have become.

~Steven Jenkins

RECIPE INDEX

CPSIA information can be obtained
at www.ICGtesting.com
Printed in the USA
BVHW02n1414260418
514432BV00002B/2/P